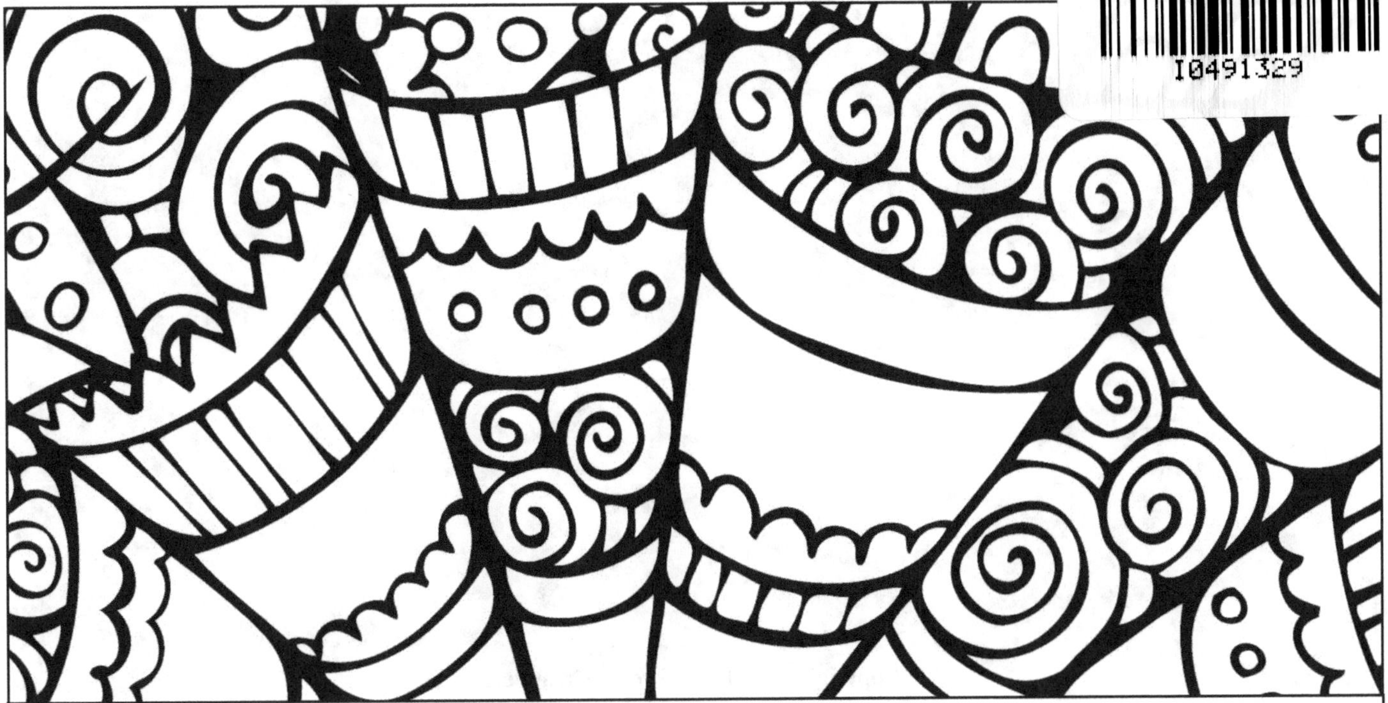

simply creative

HALLOWEEN

coloring book for adults

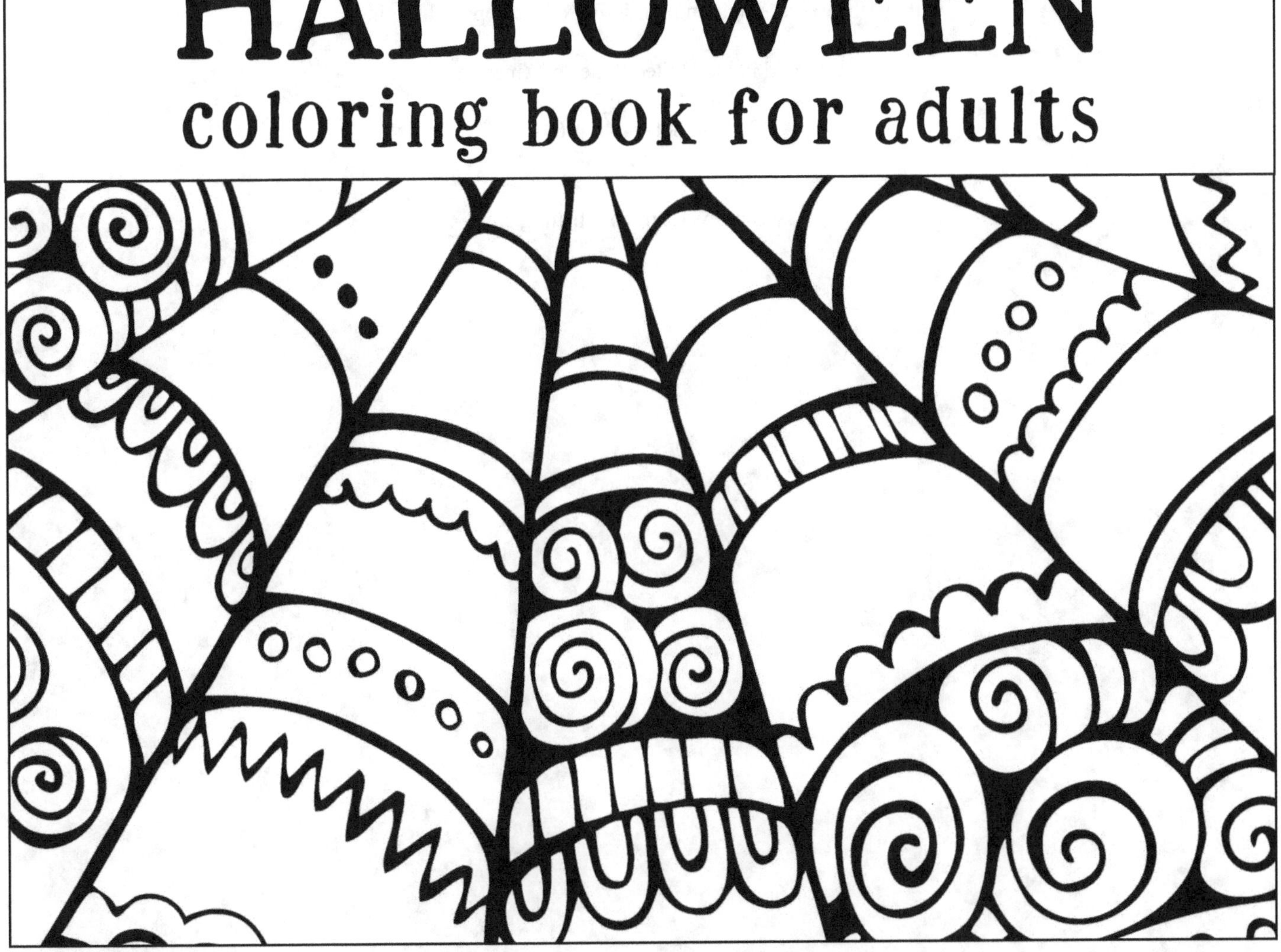

Design by Lynne Dempsey
Art courtesy of Creative Market, 123RF, Shutterstock, Storyblocks, and The Hungry JPEG.

Printed in the United States of America
First Printing 2017
ISBN 978-1-944474-04-1

www.simplycreativepublishing.com

This book belongs to:

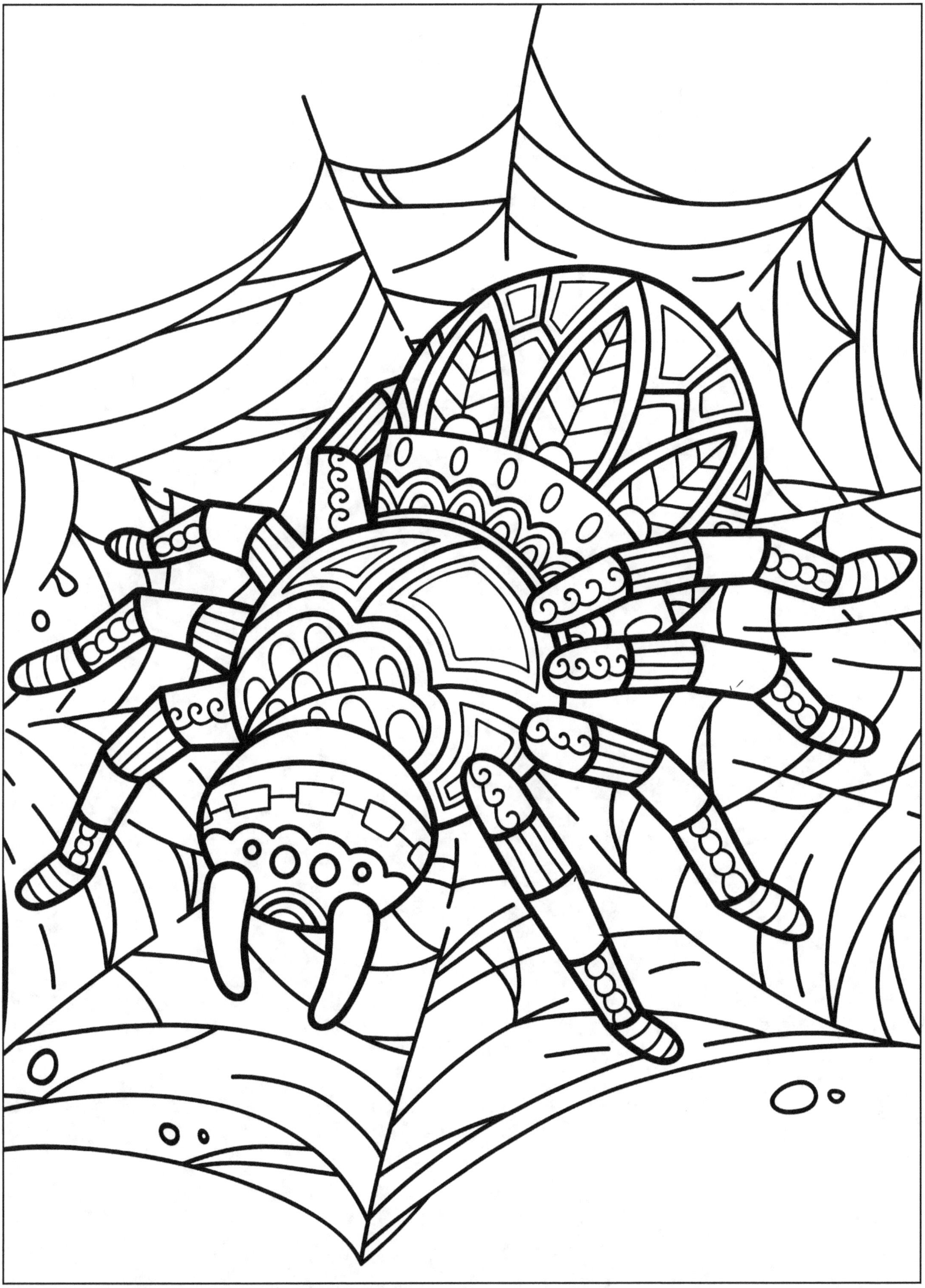

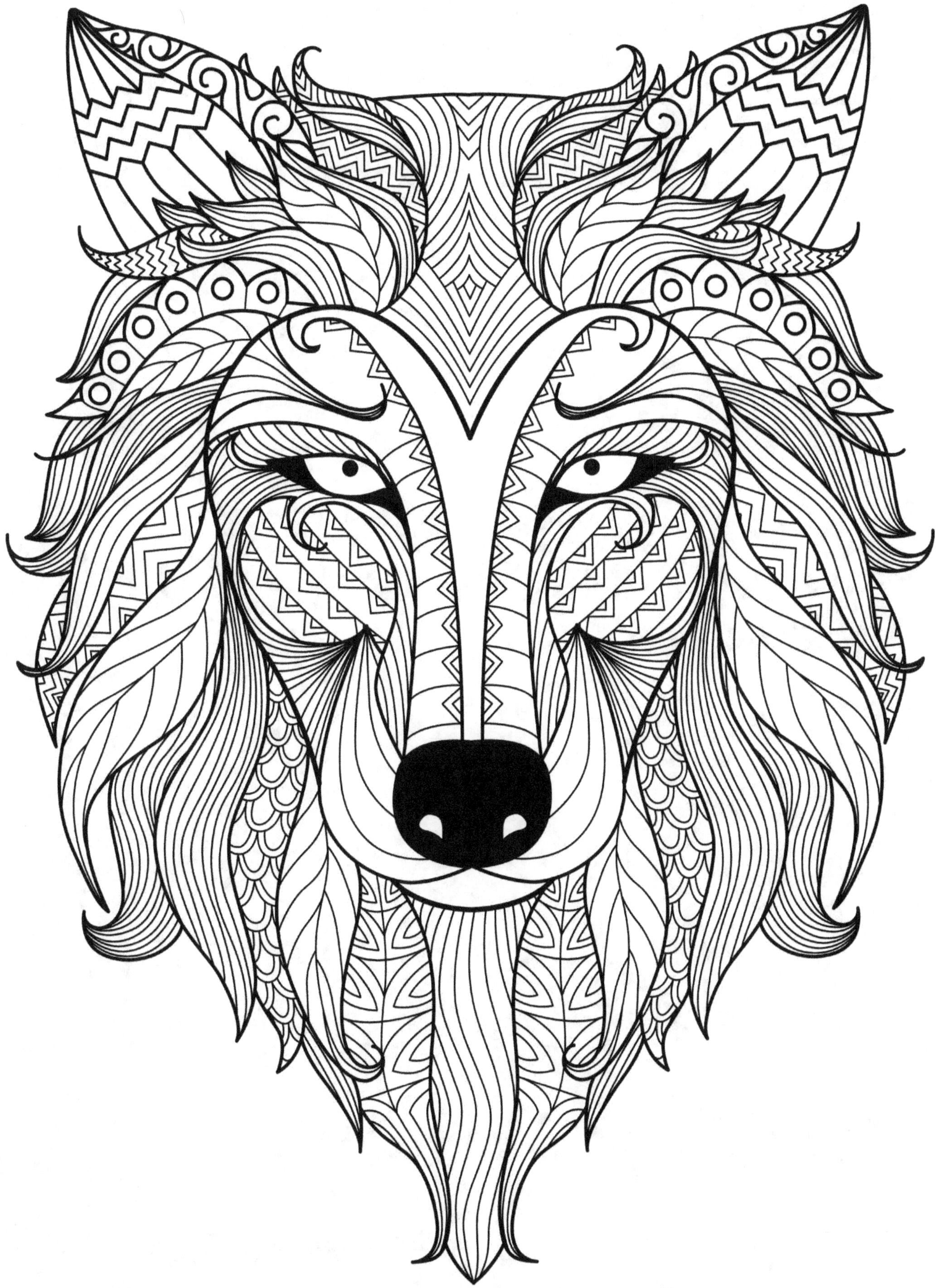

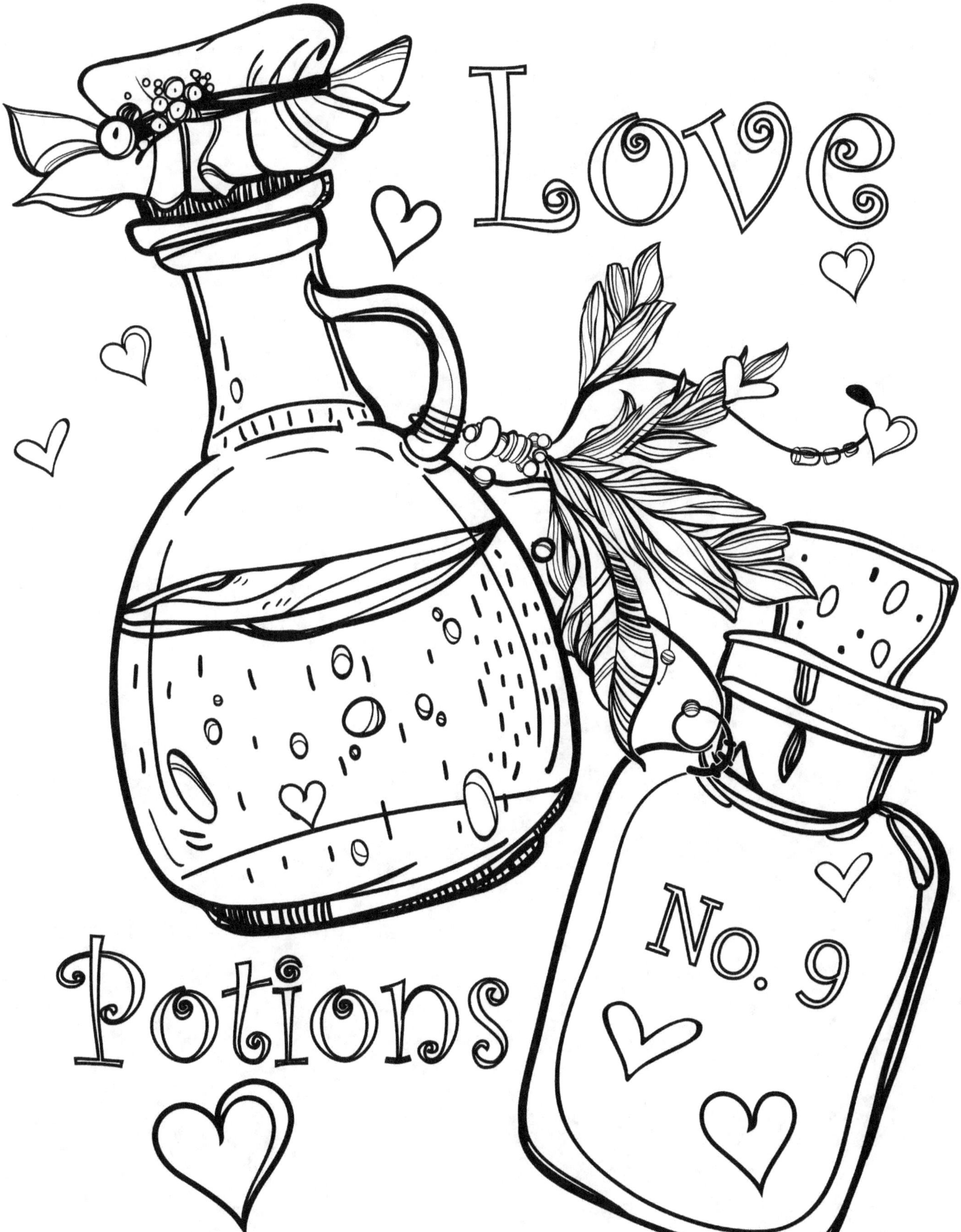
Love
Potions
No. 9

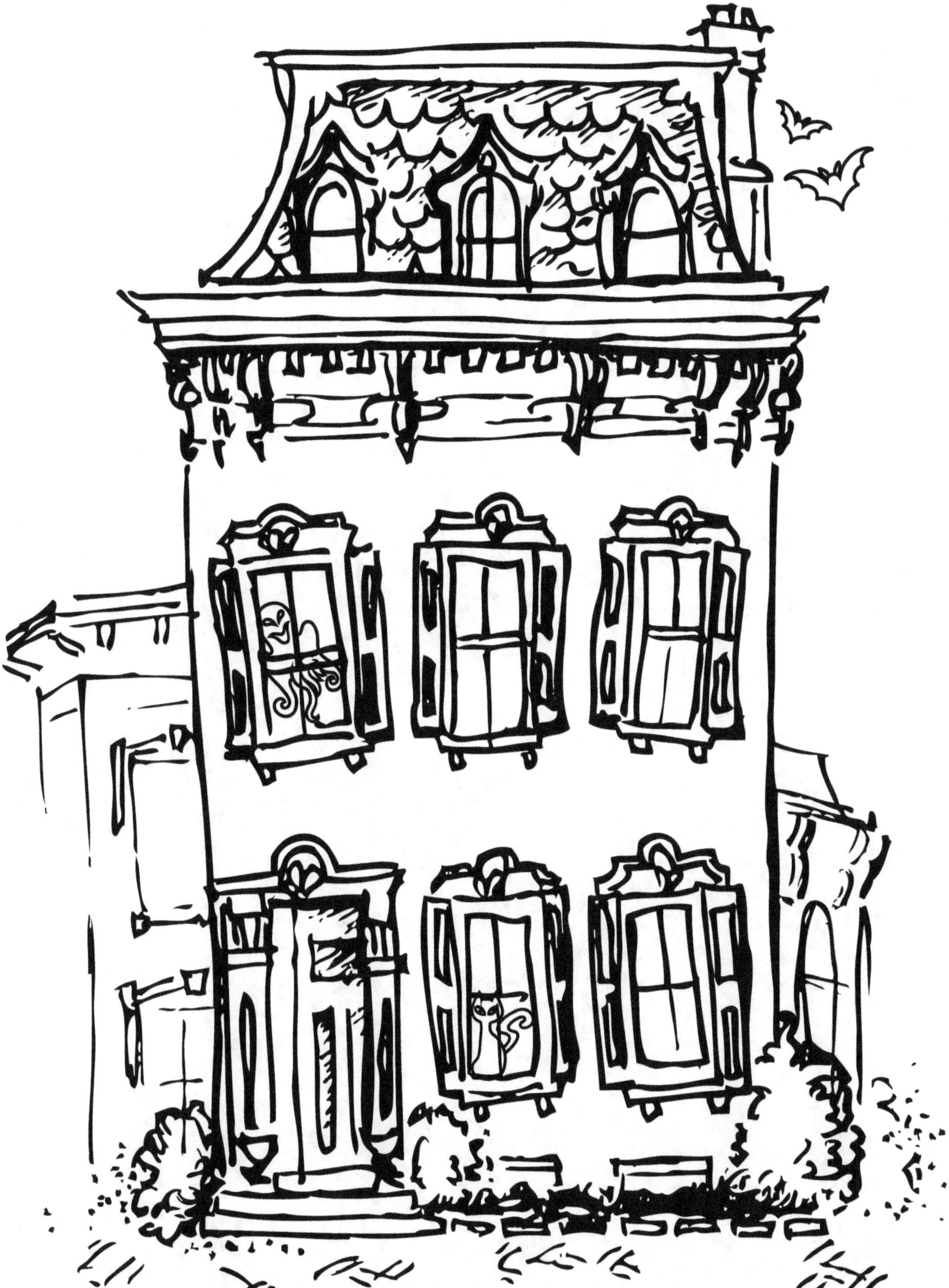

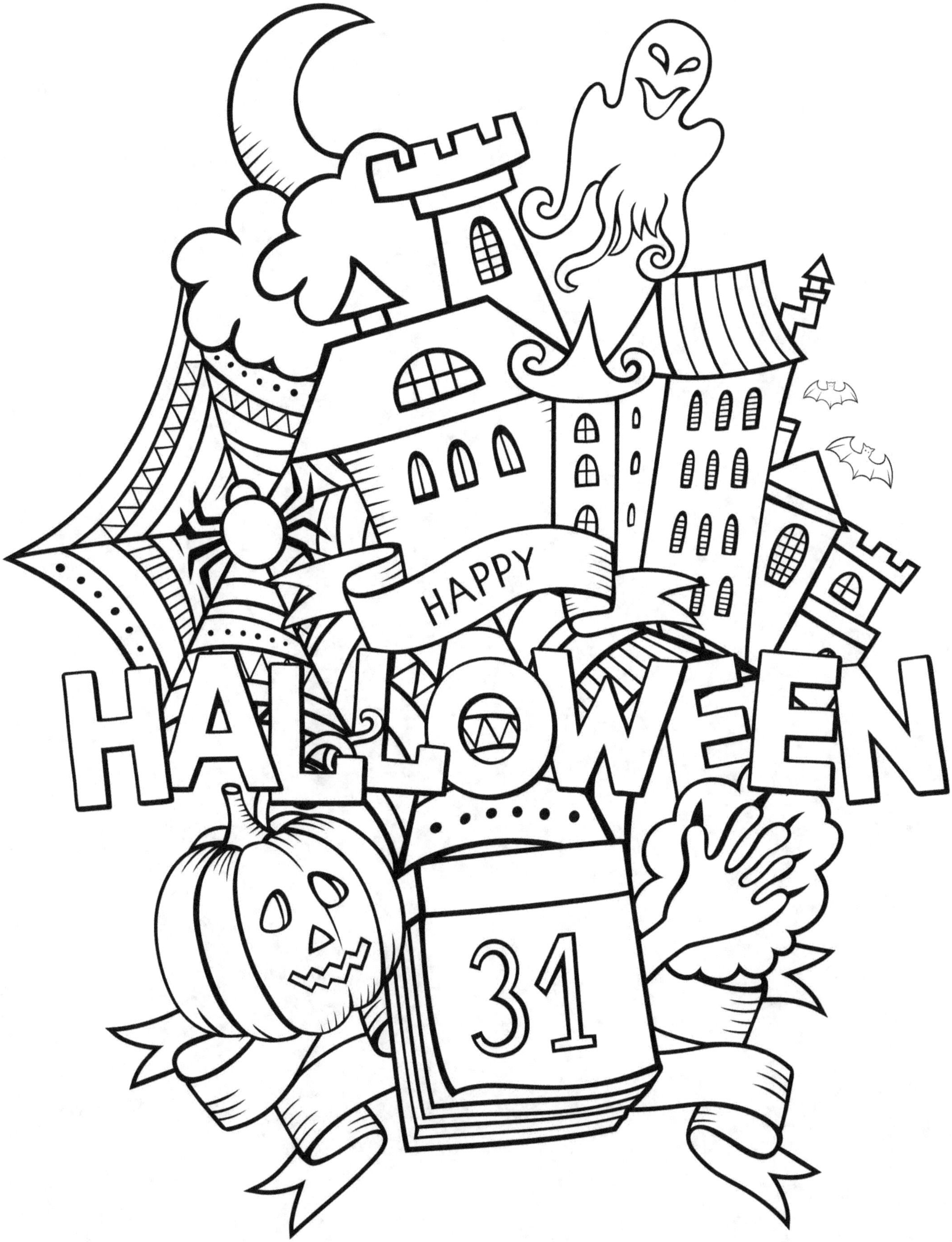
HAPPY
HALLOWEEN
31

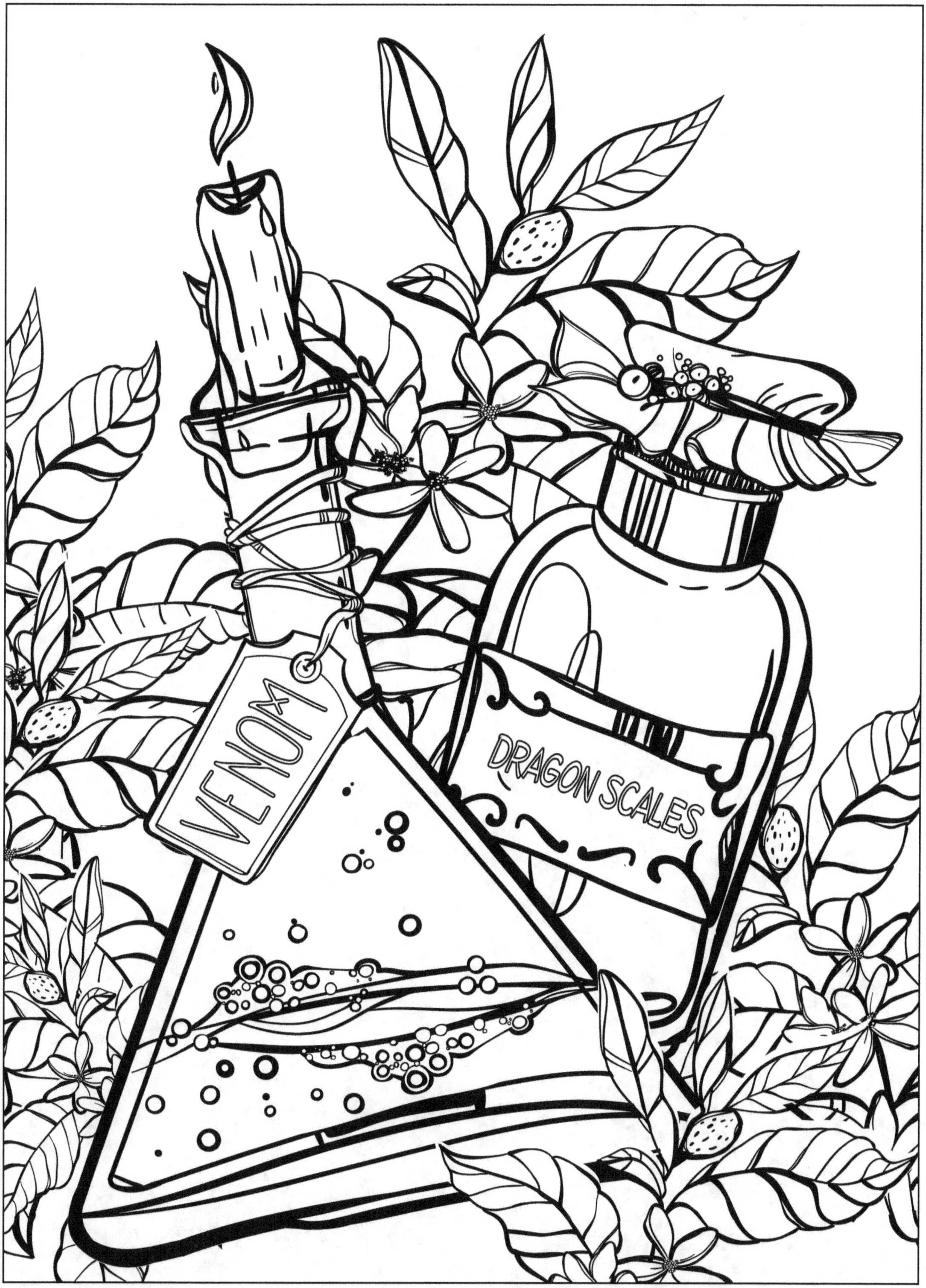
VENOM
DRAGON SCALES

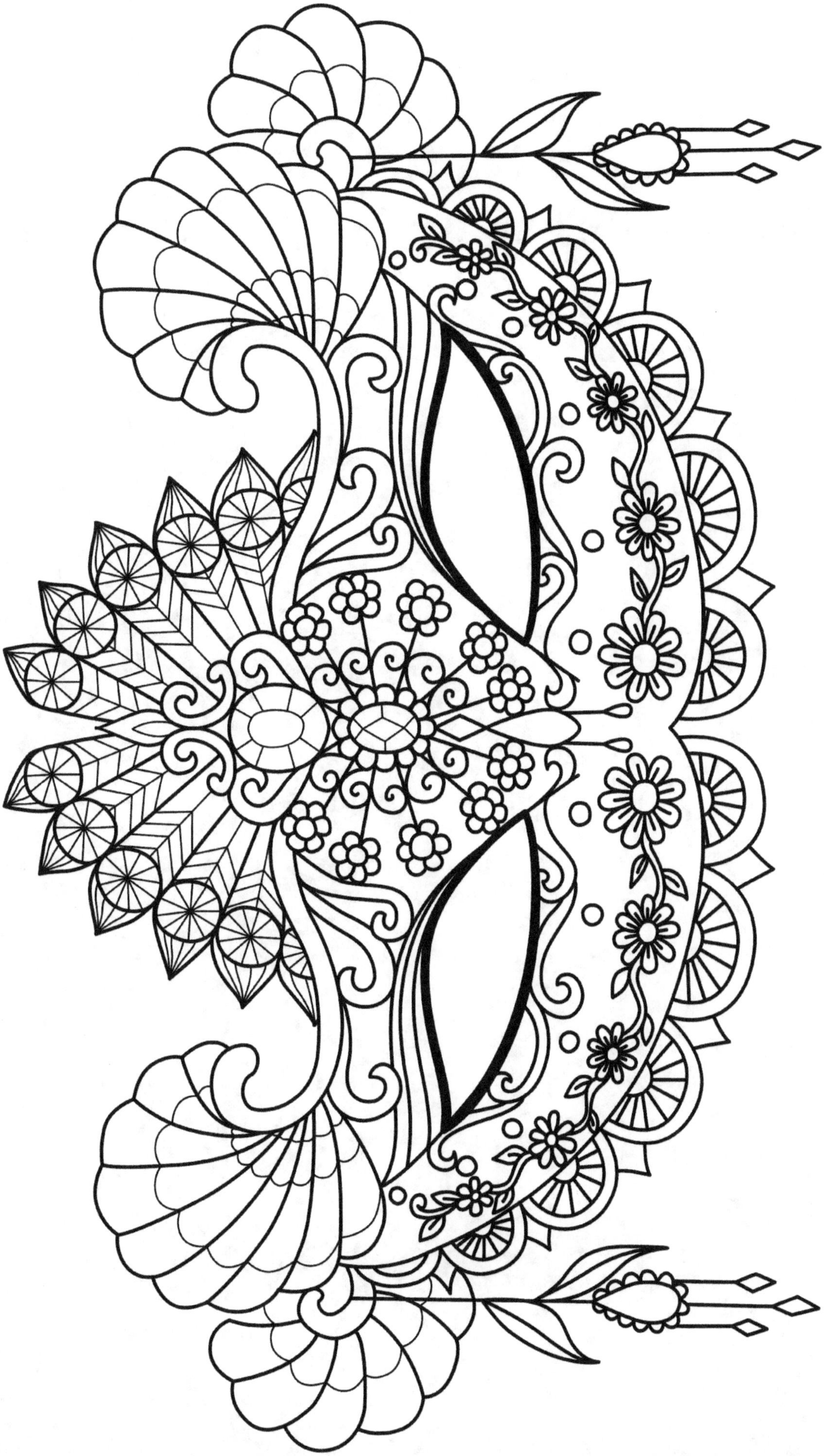

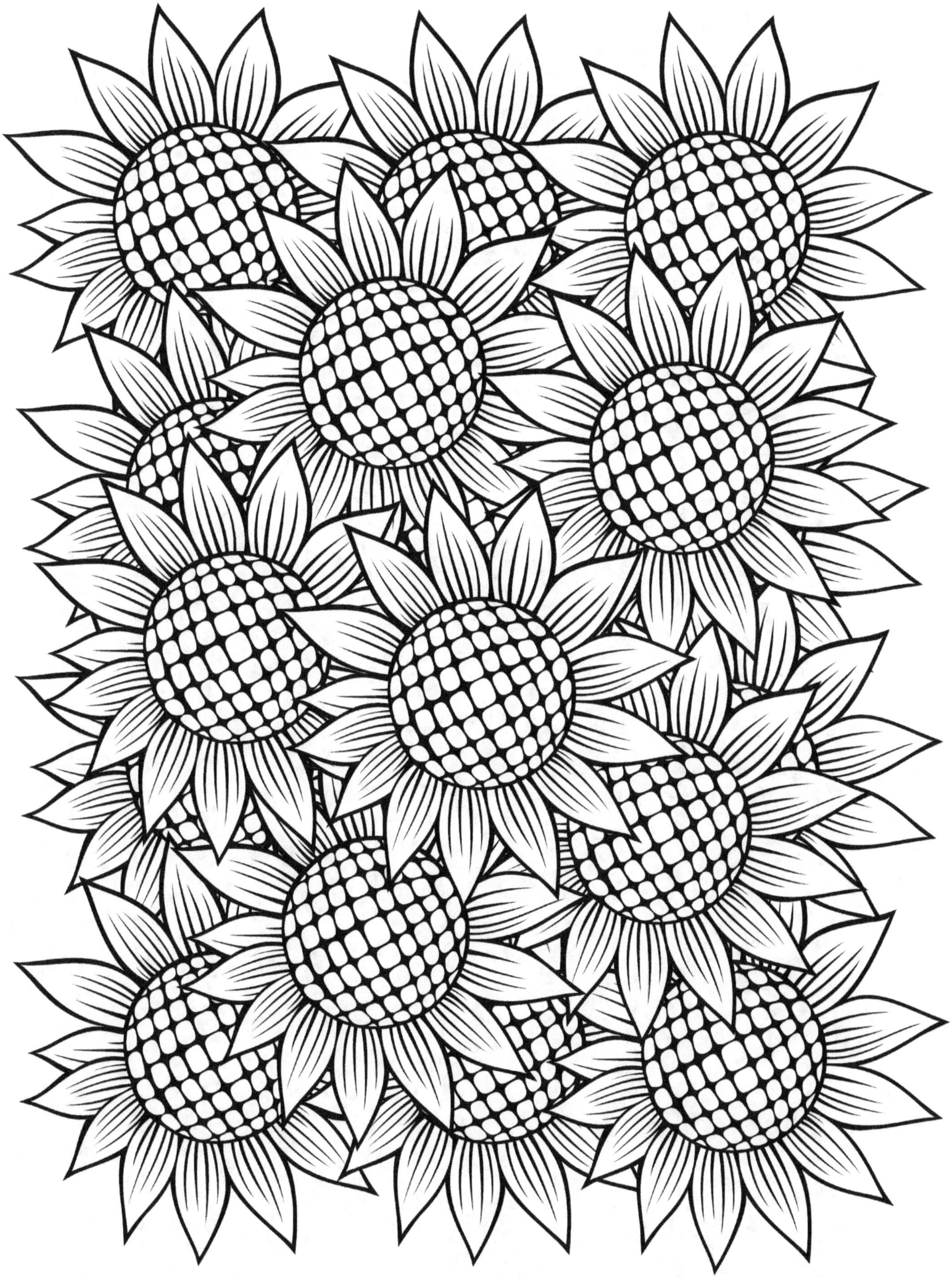

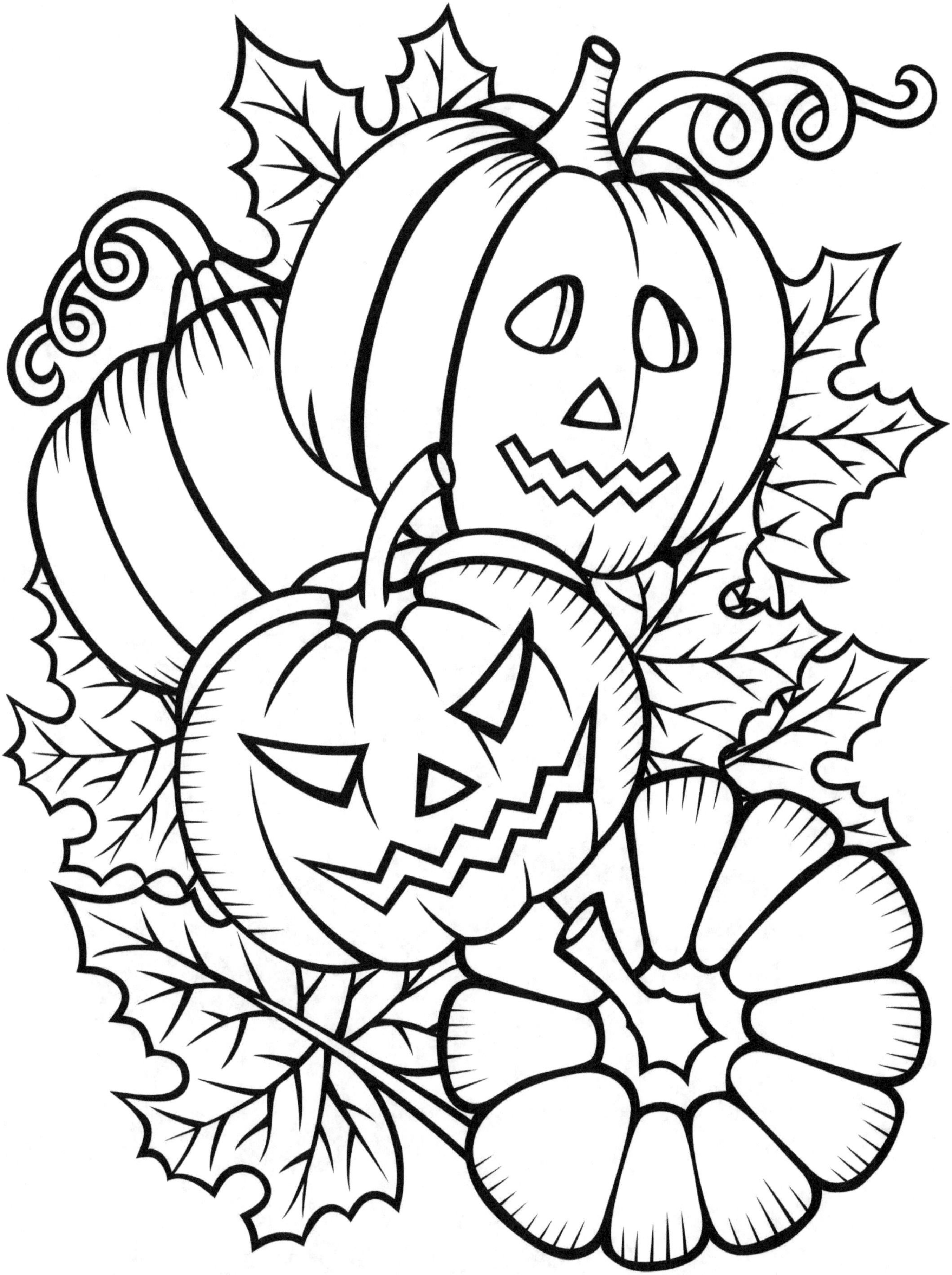

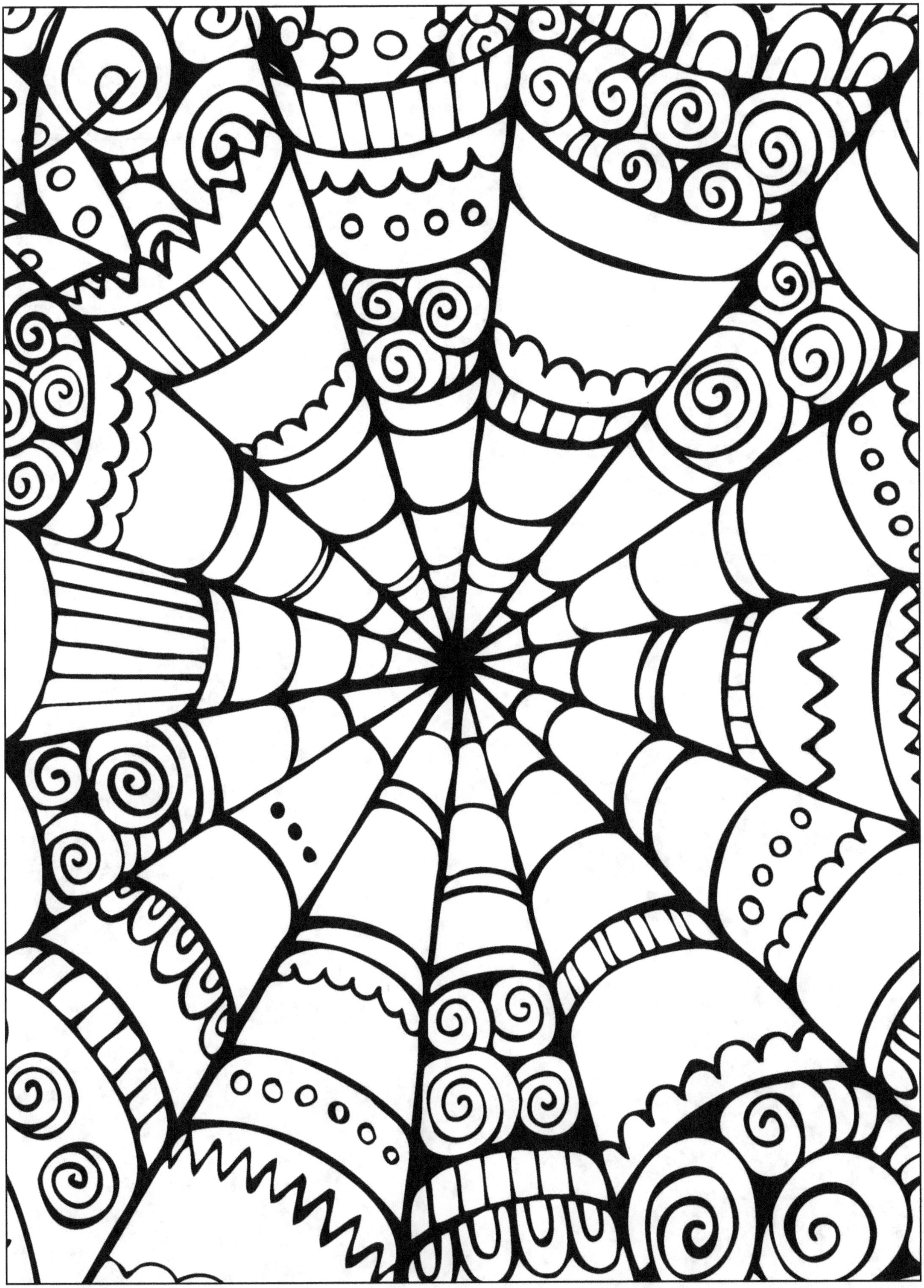

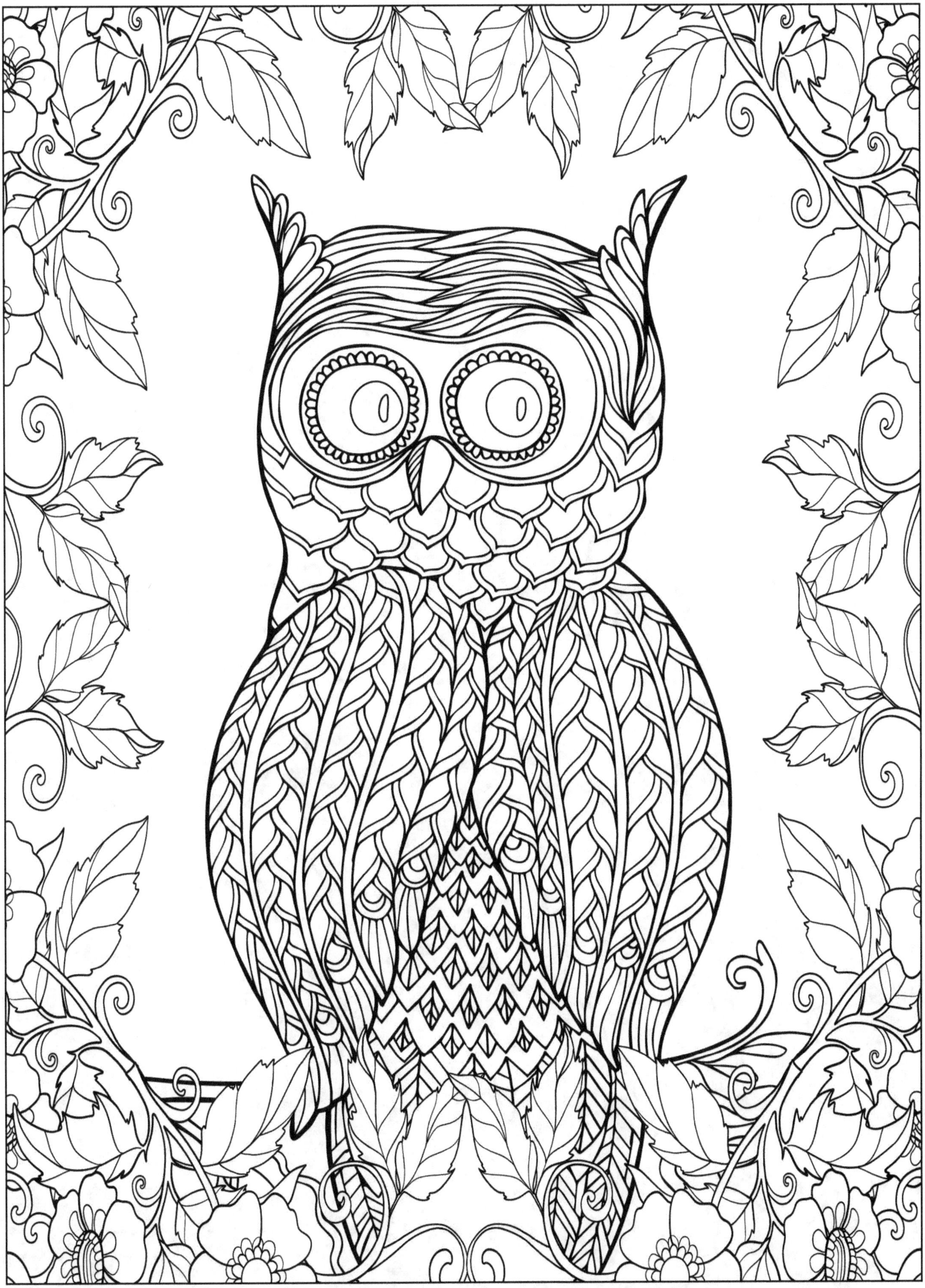

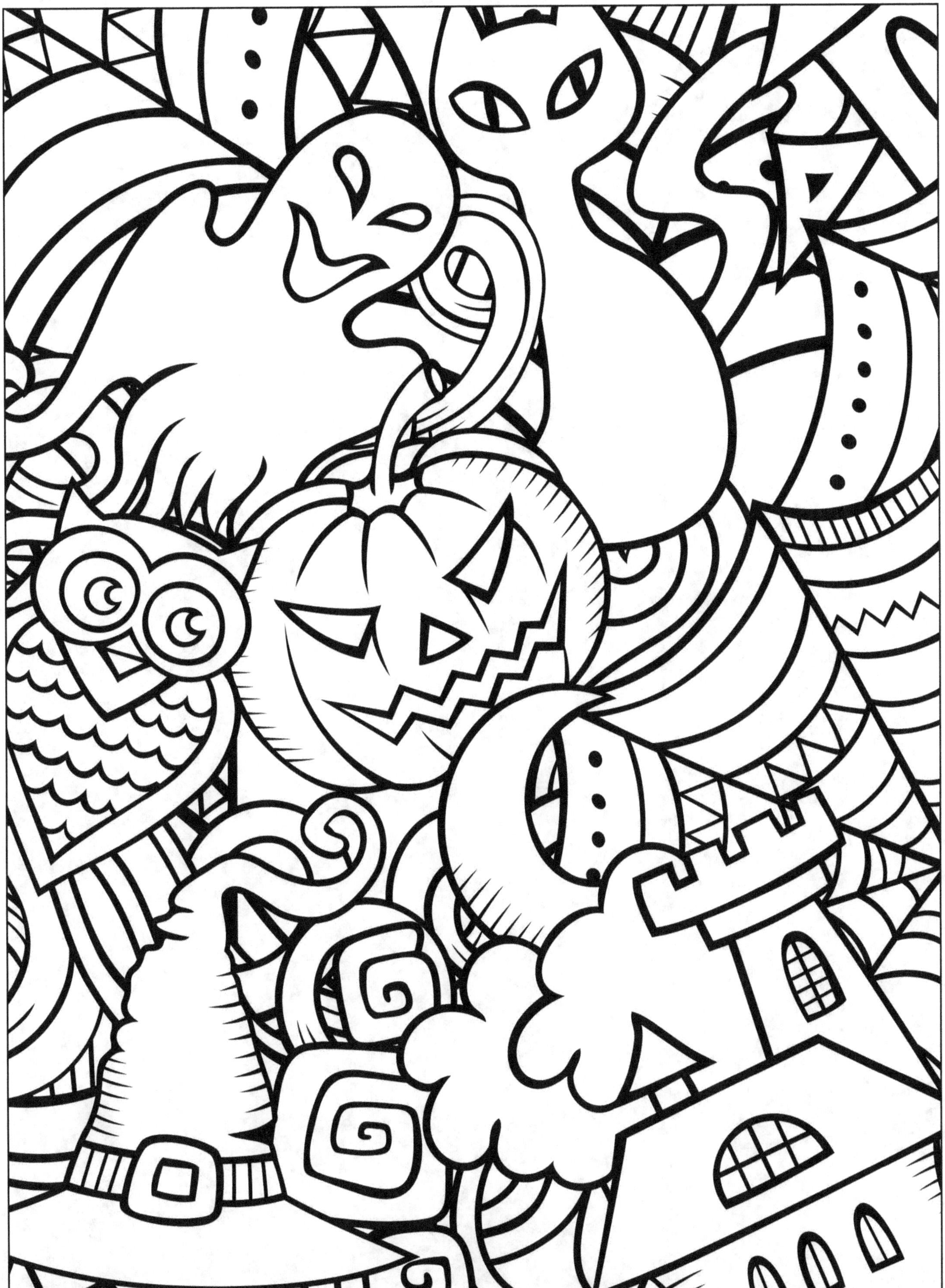

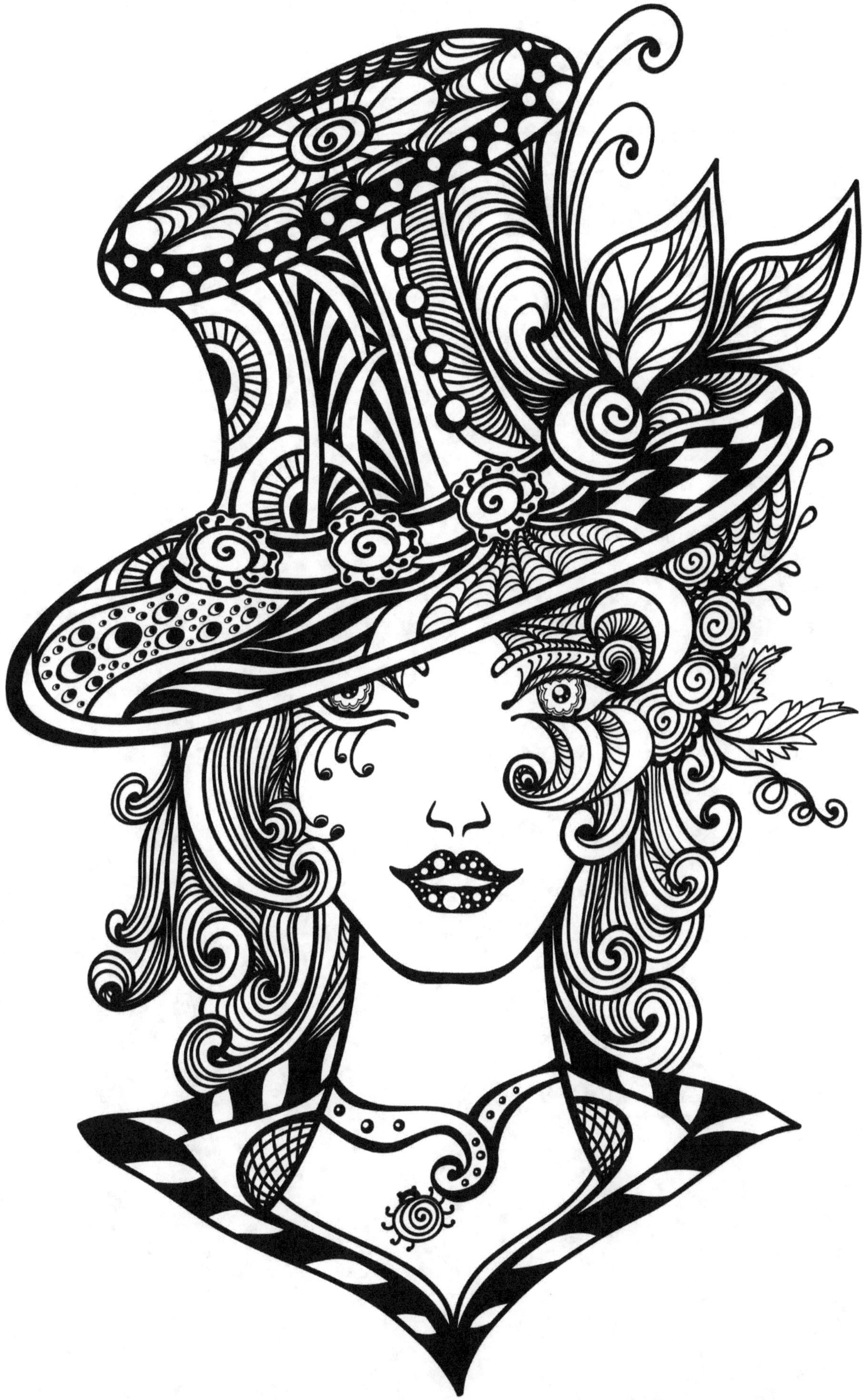

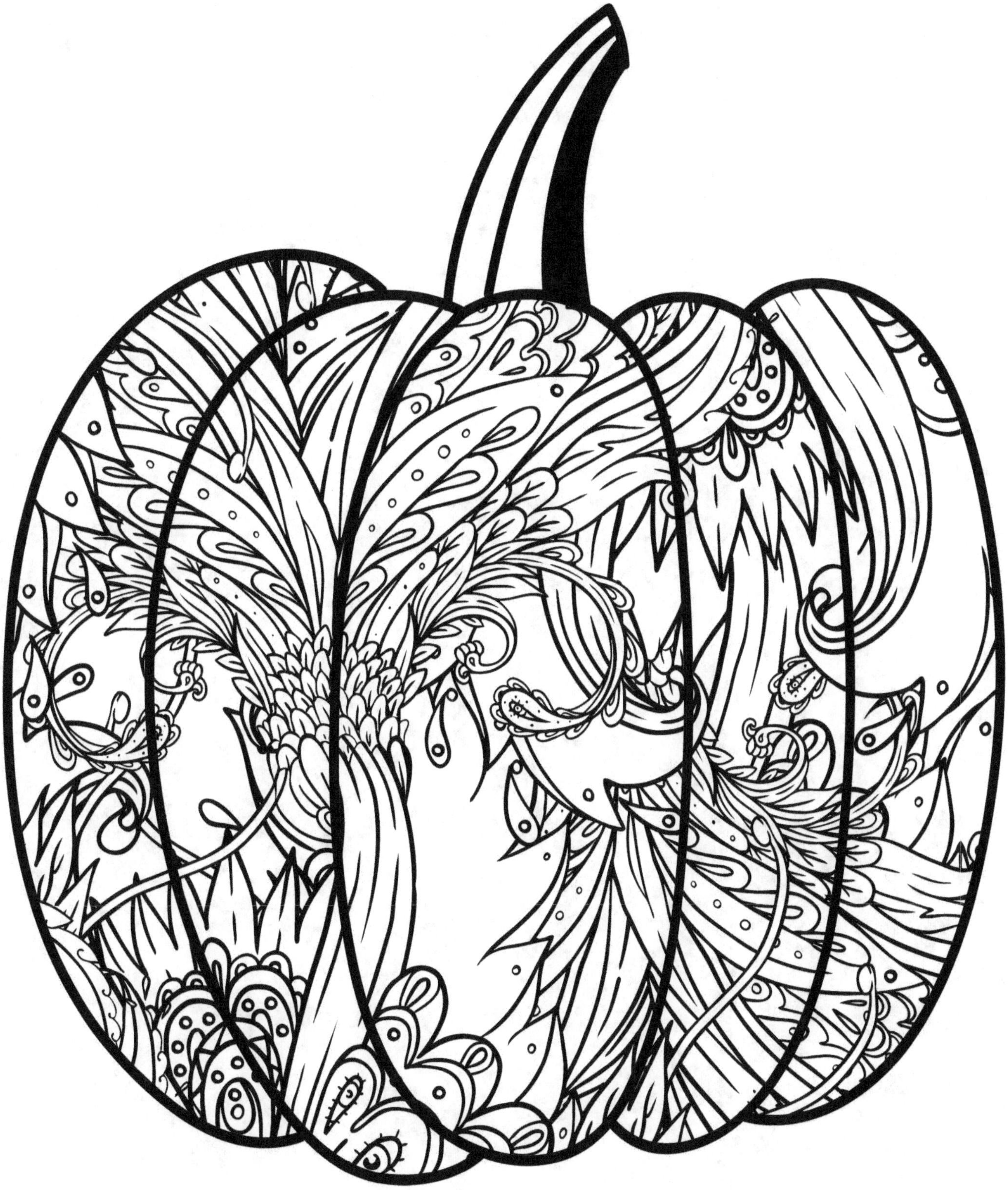

Trick
or
Treat

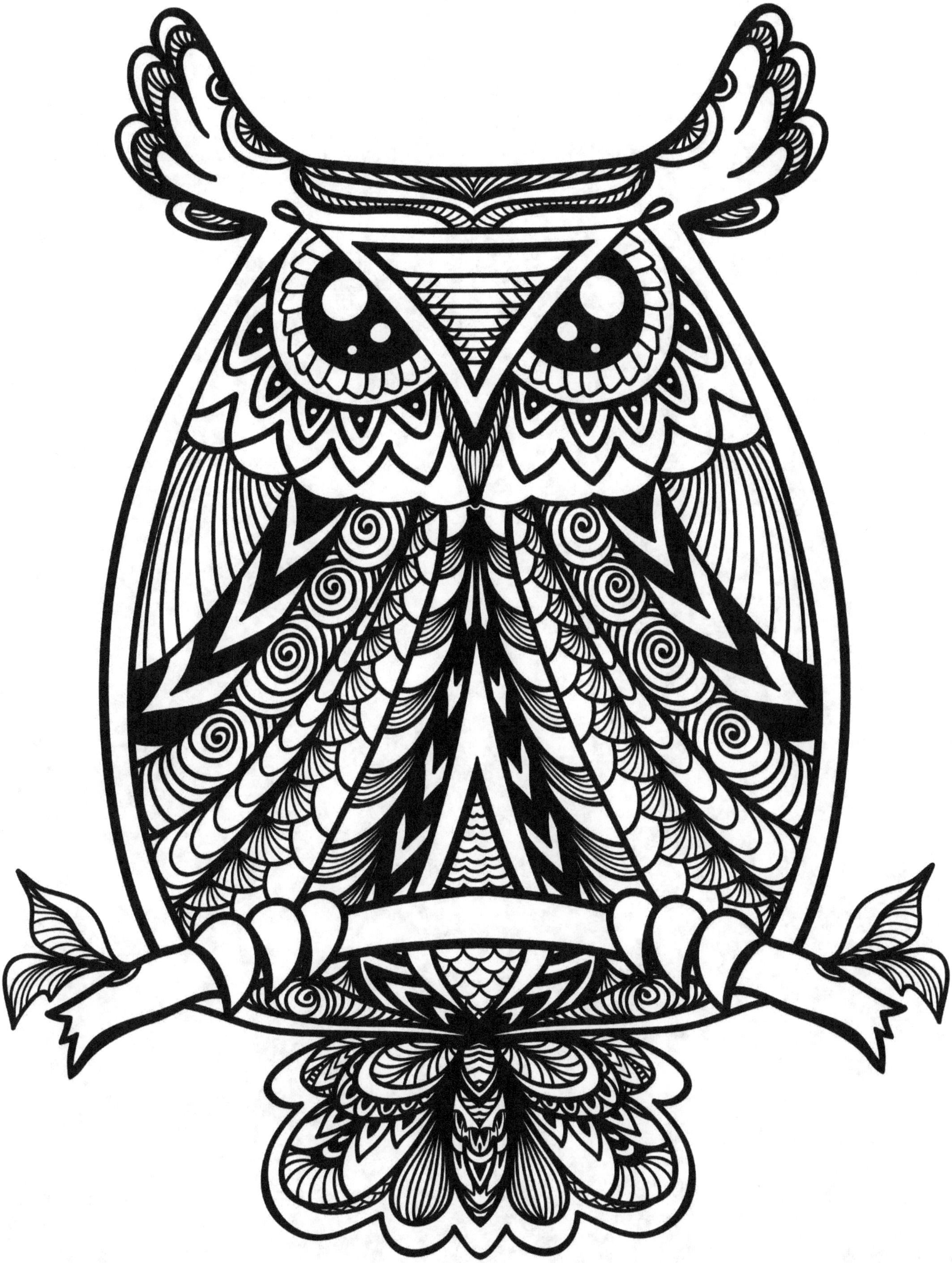

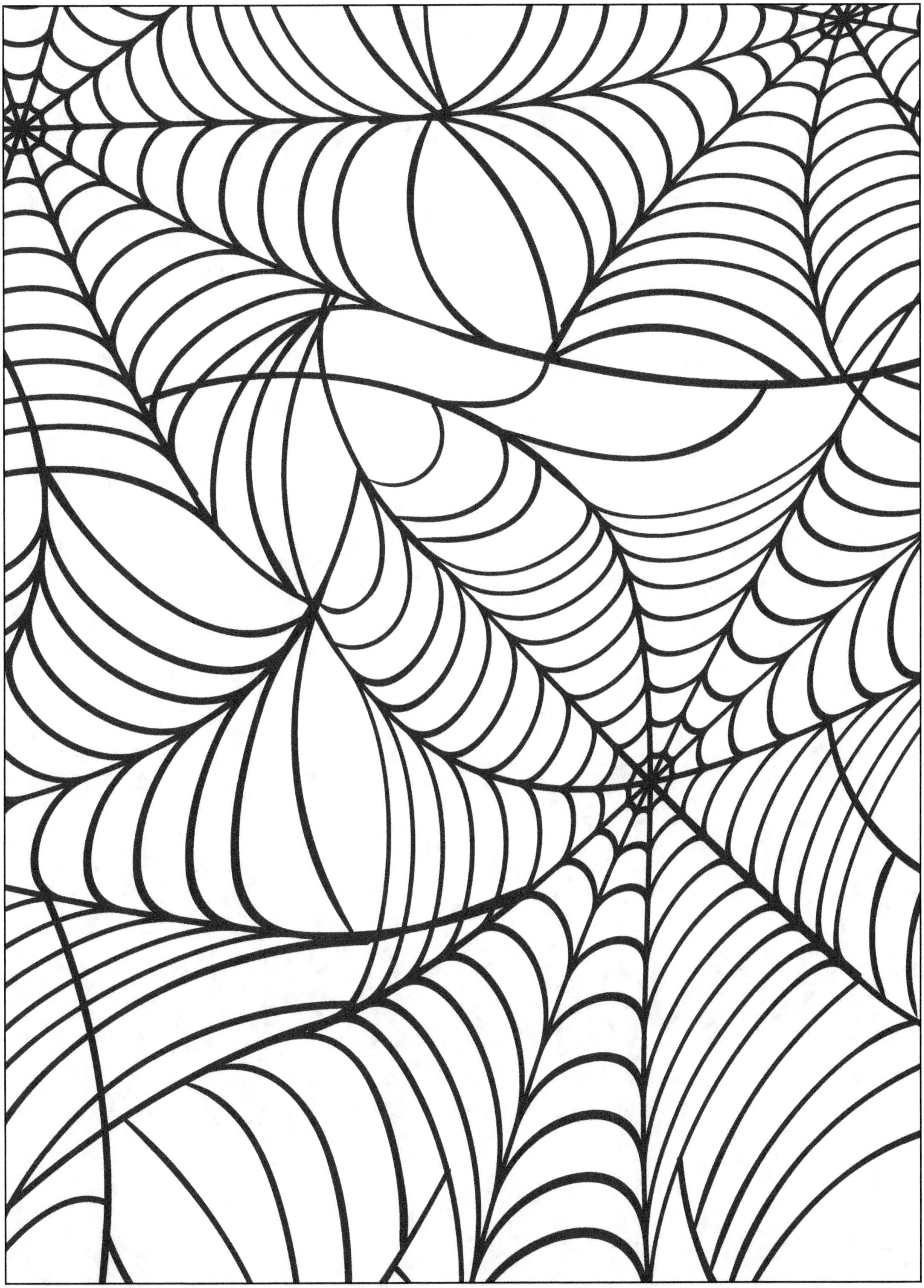

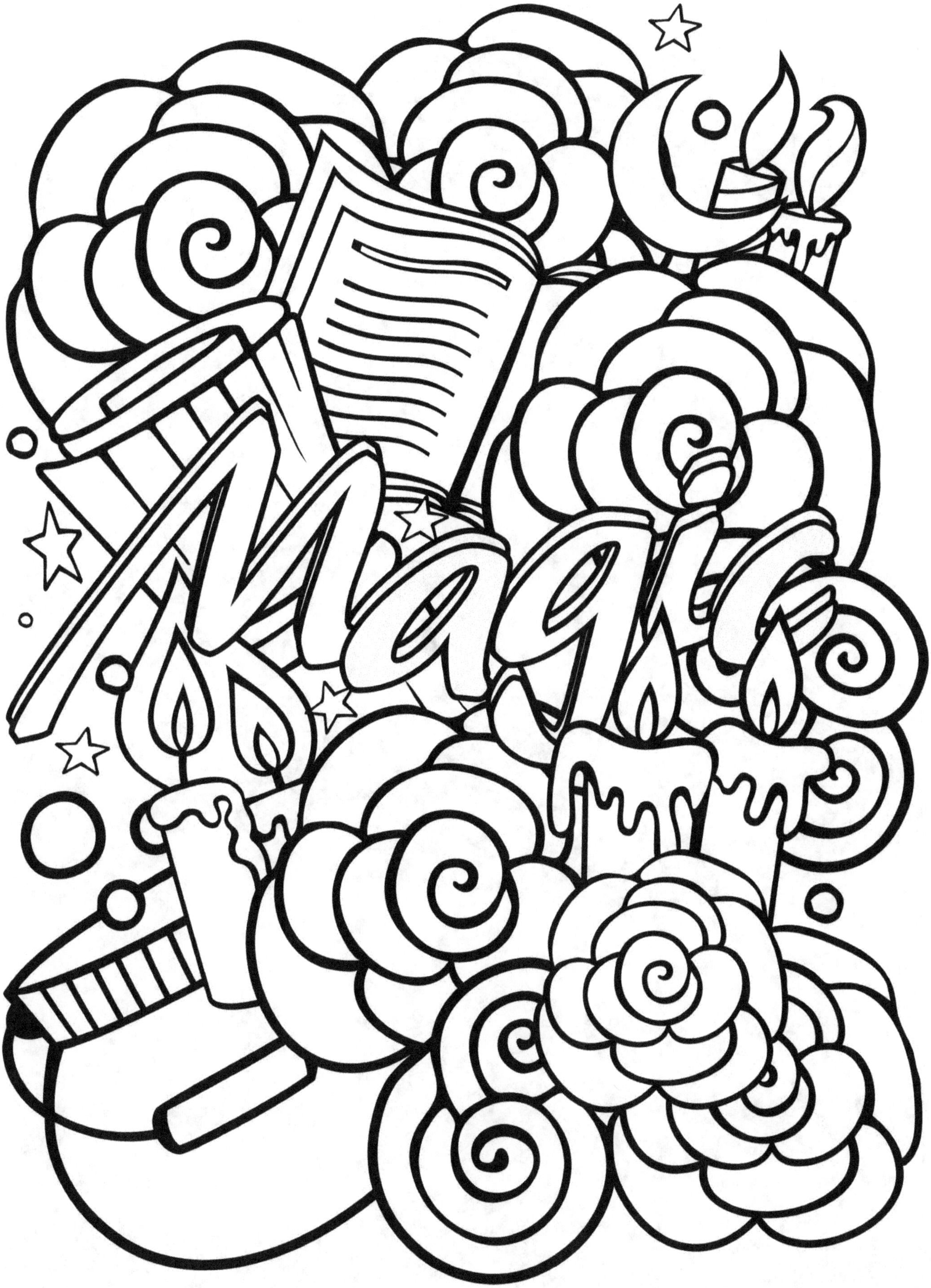
Magic

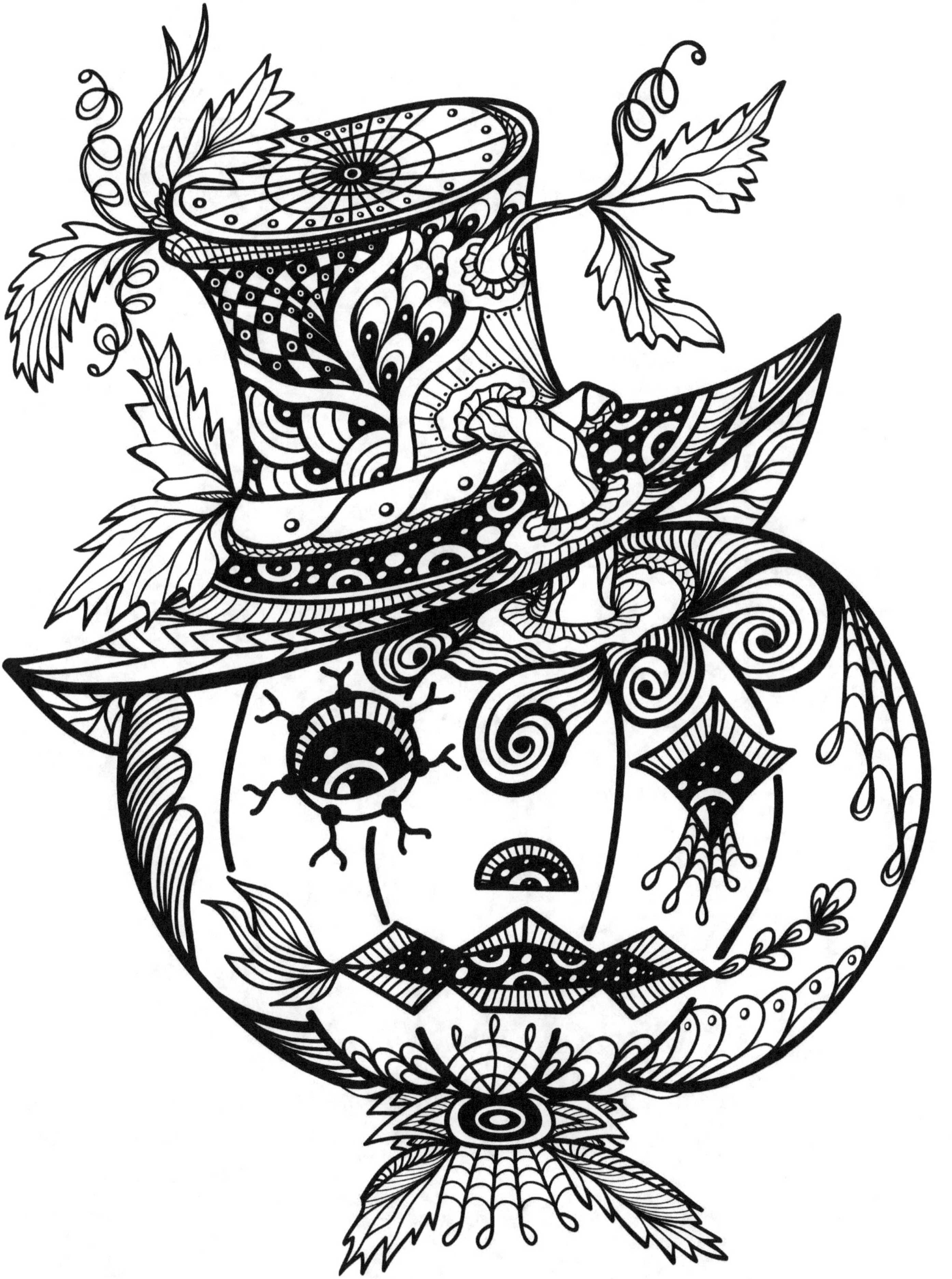

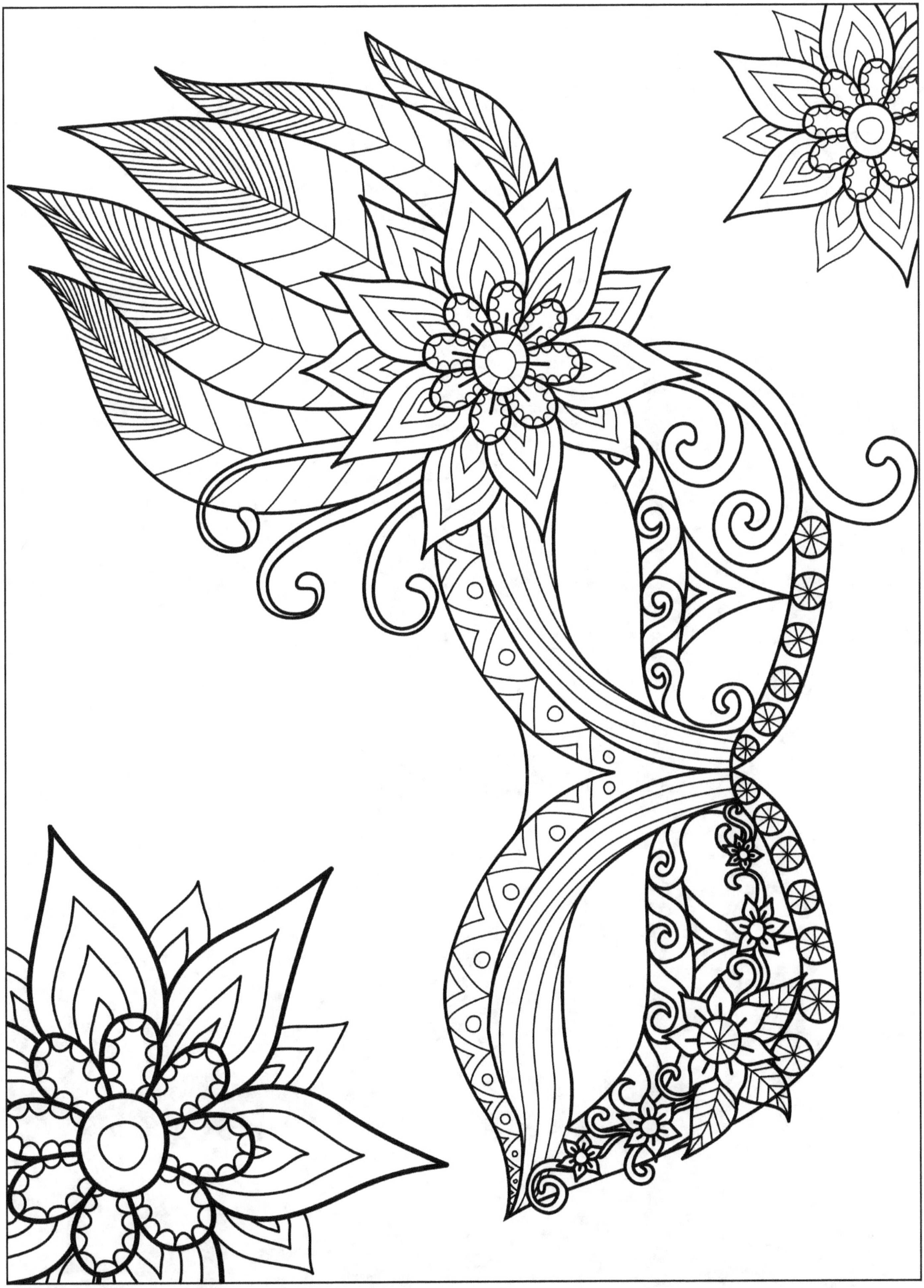

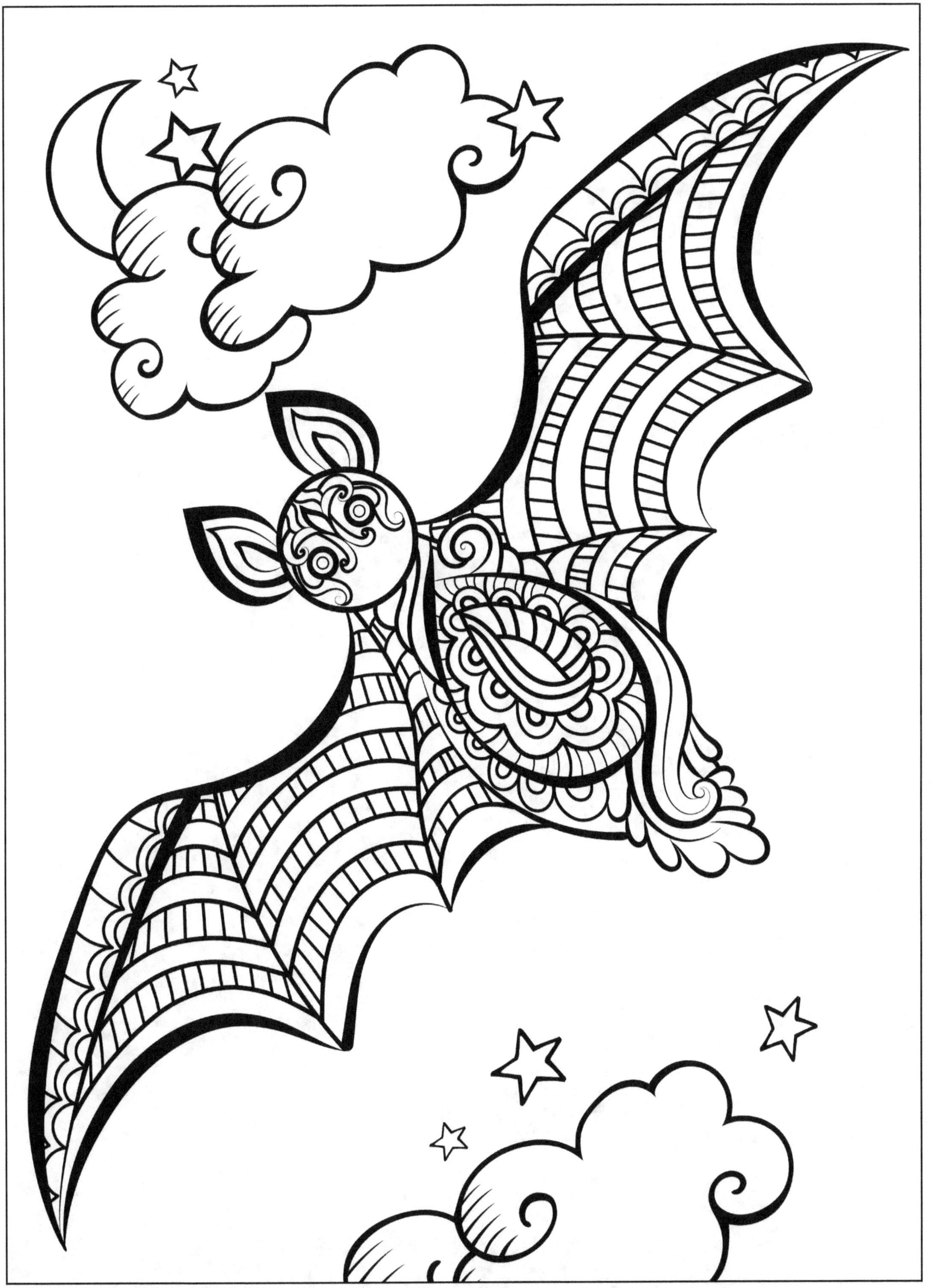

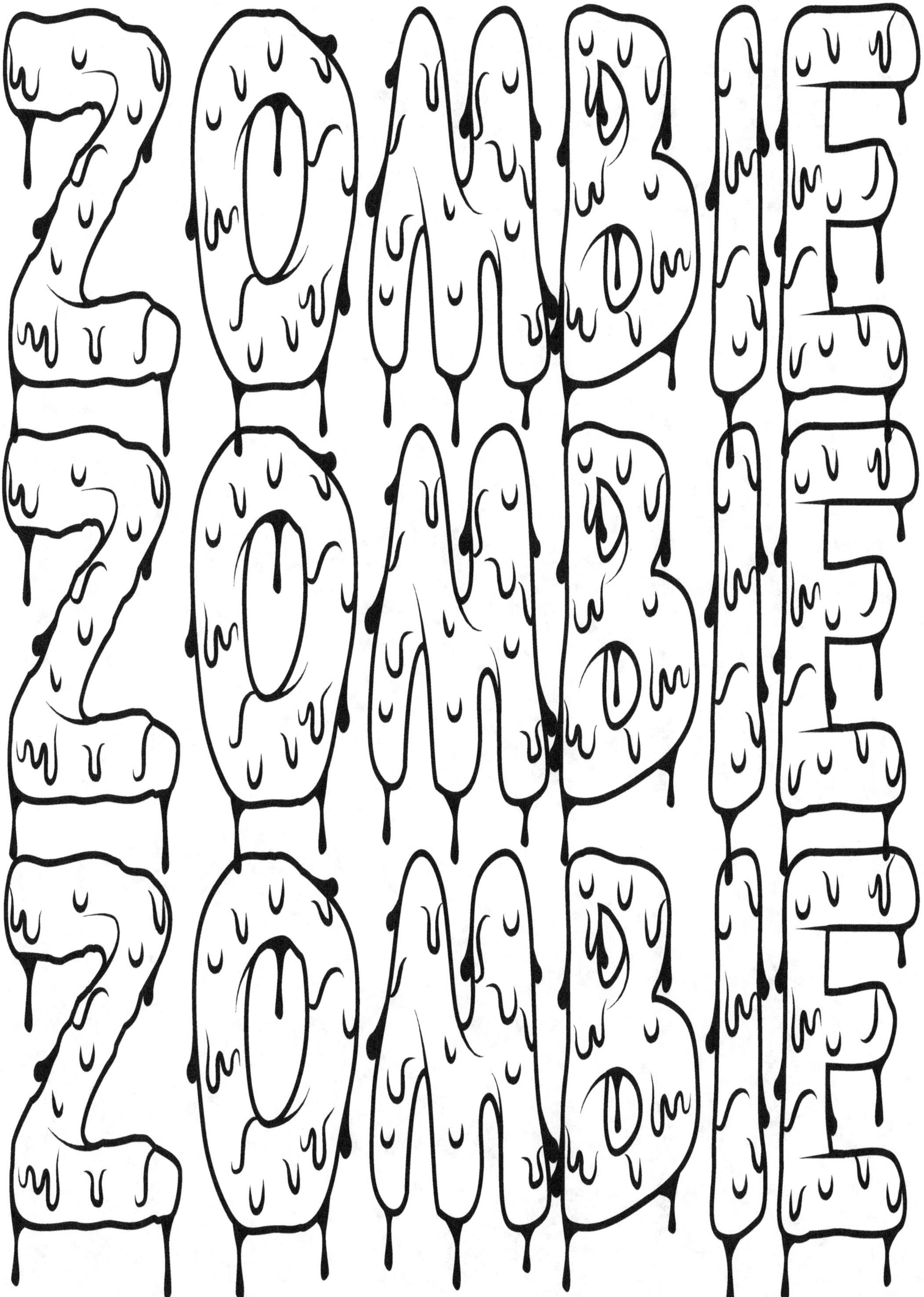
ZOMBIE
ZOMBIE
ZOMBIE

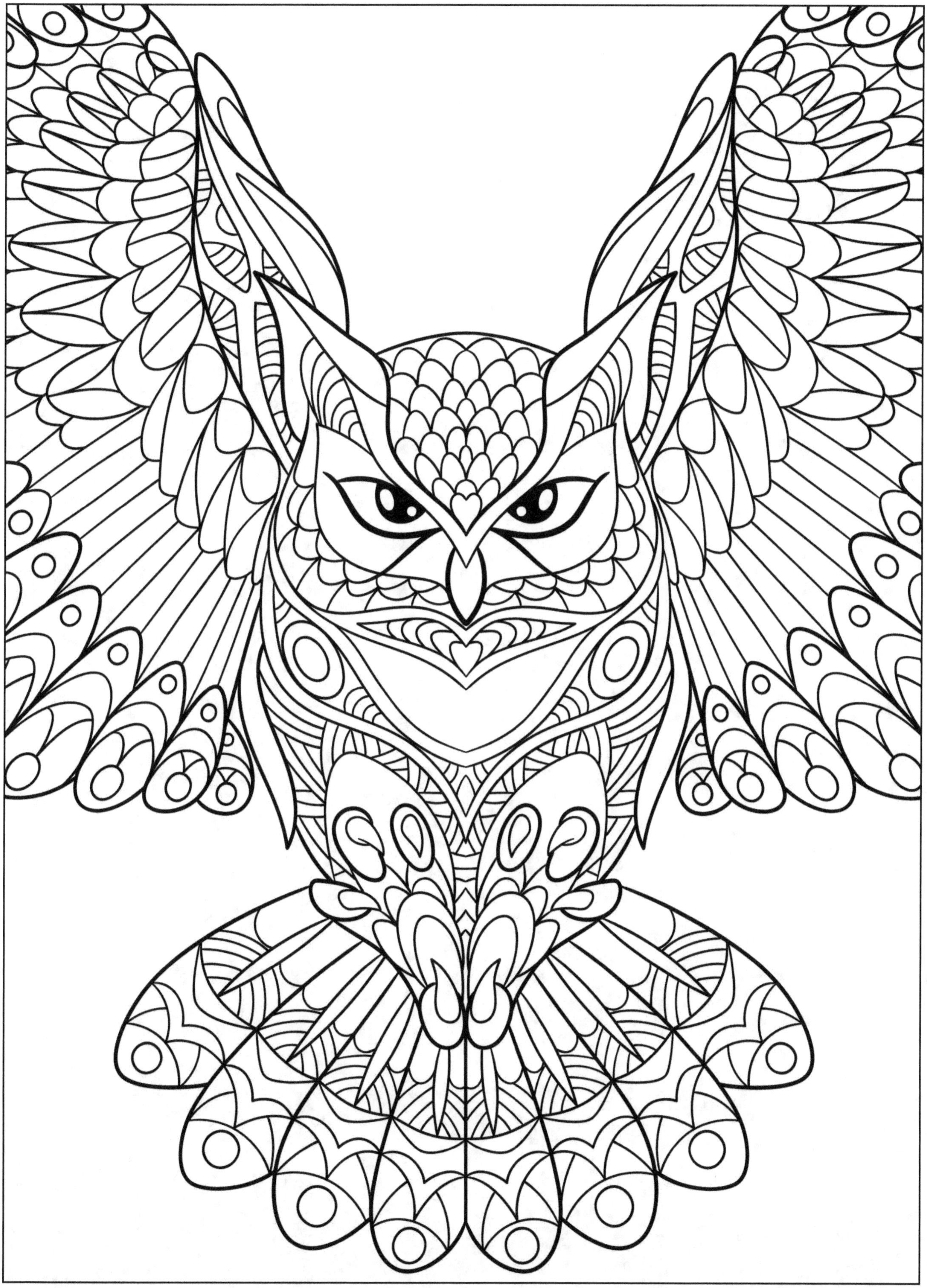

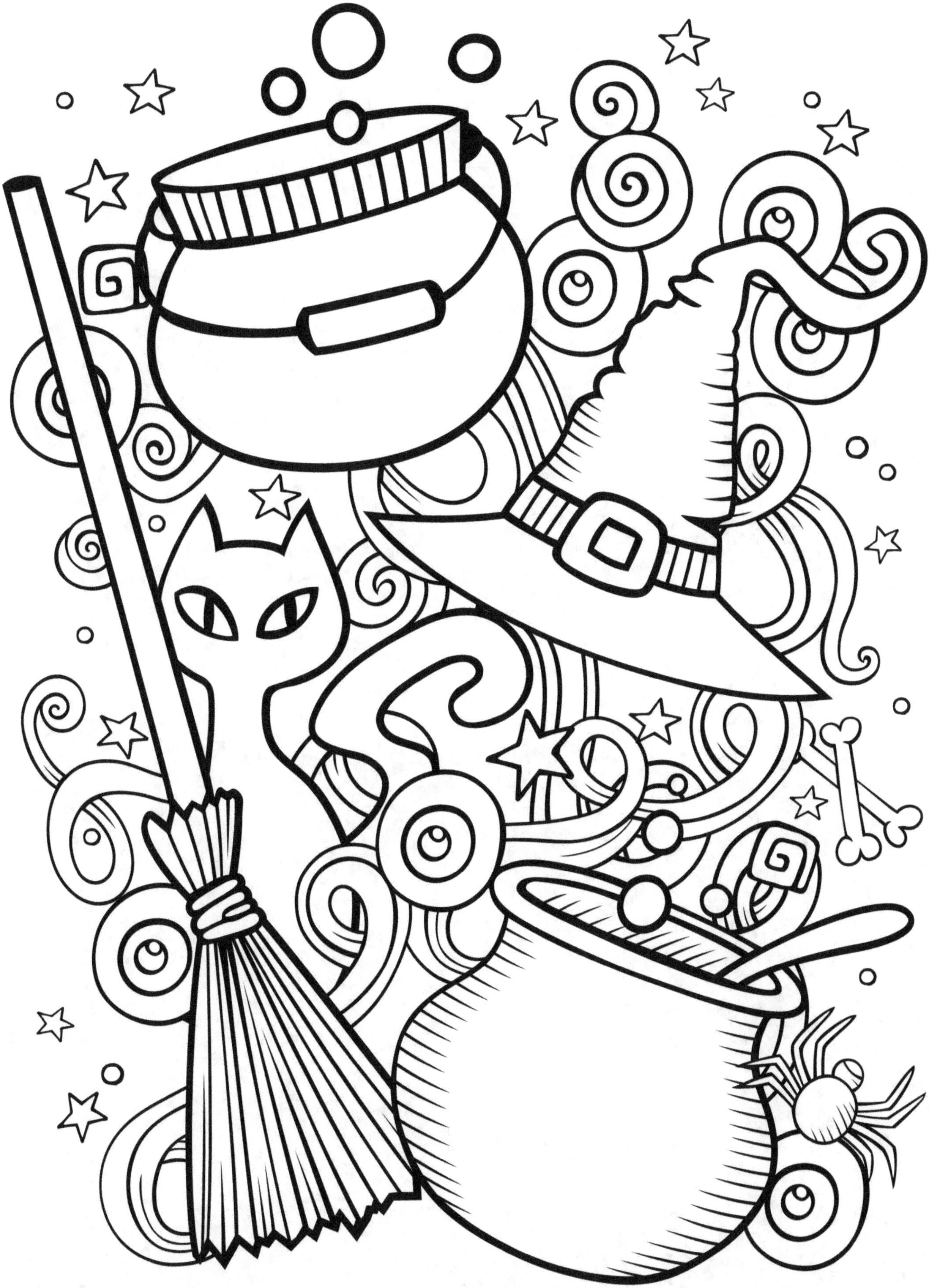

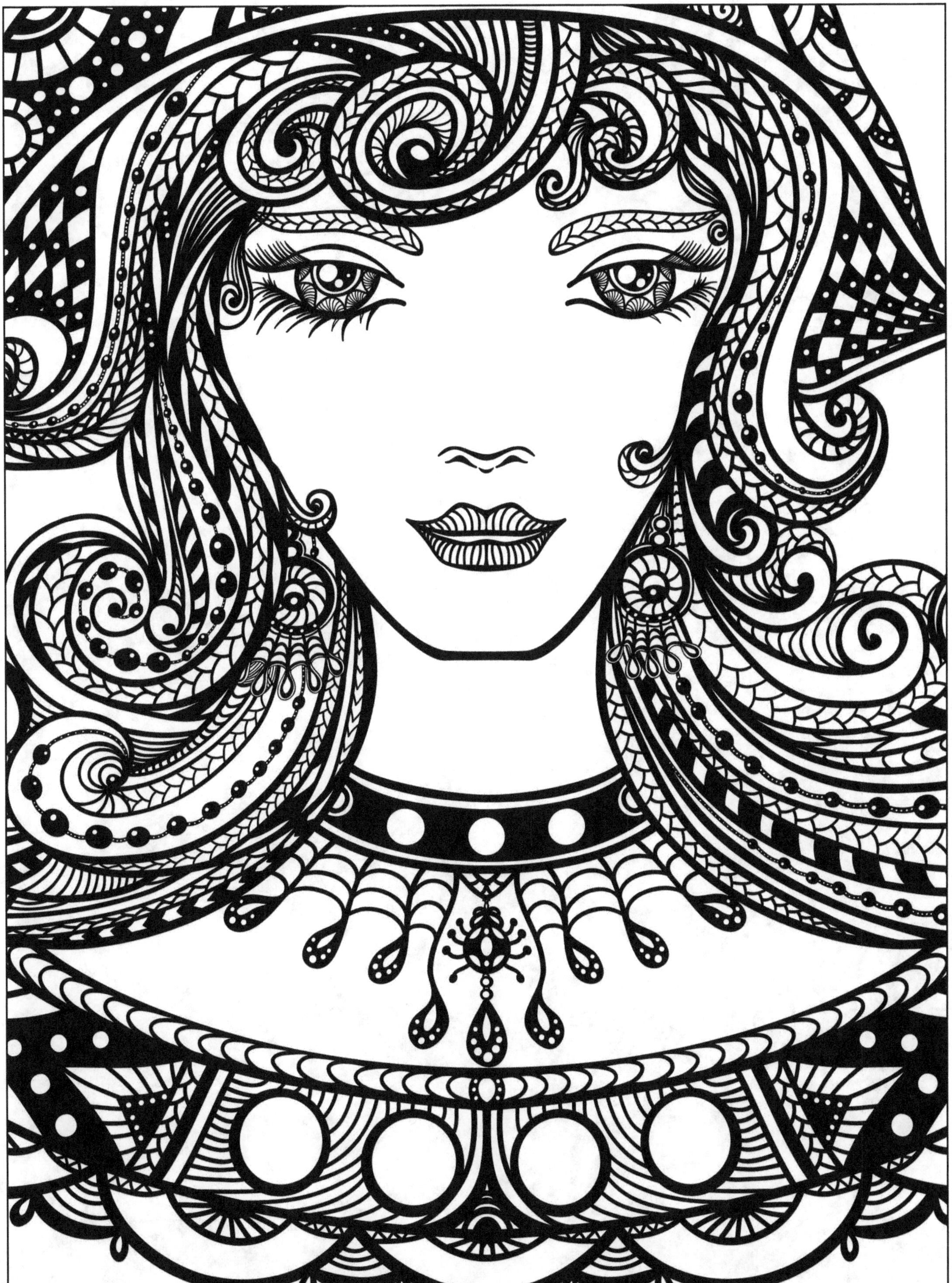

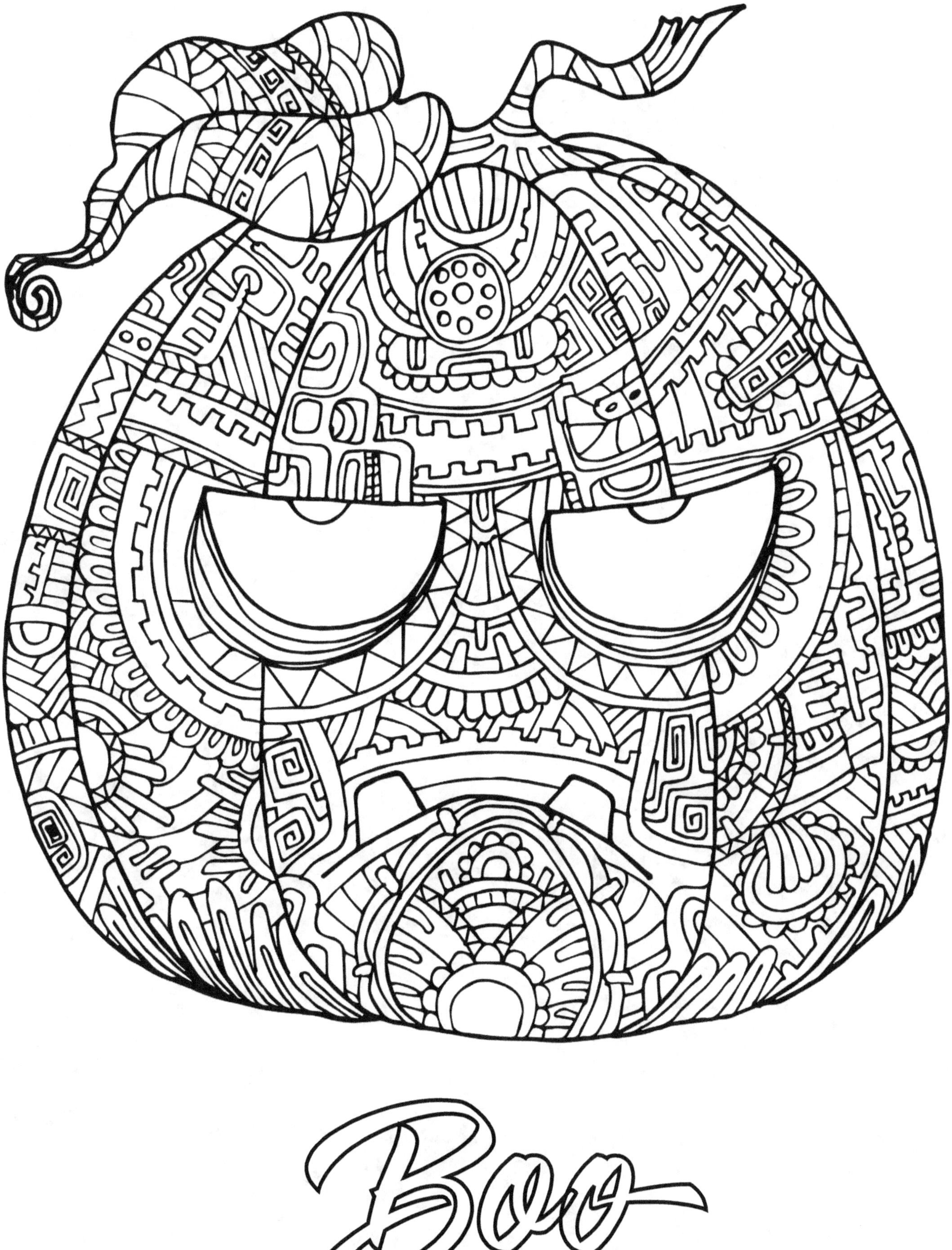
Boo

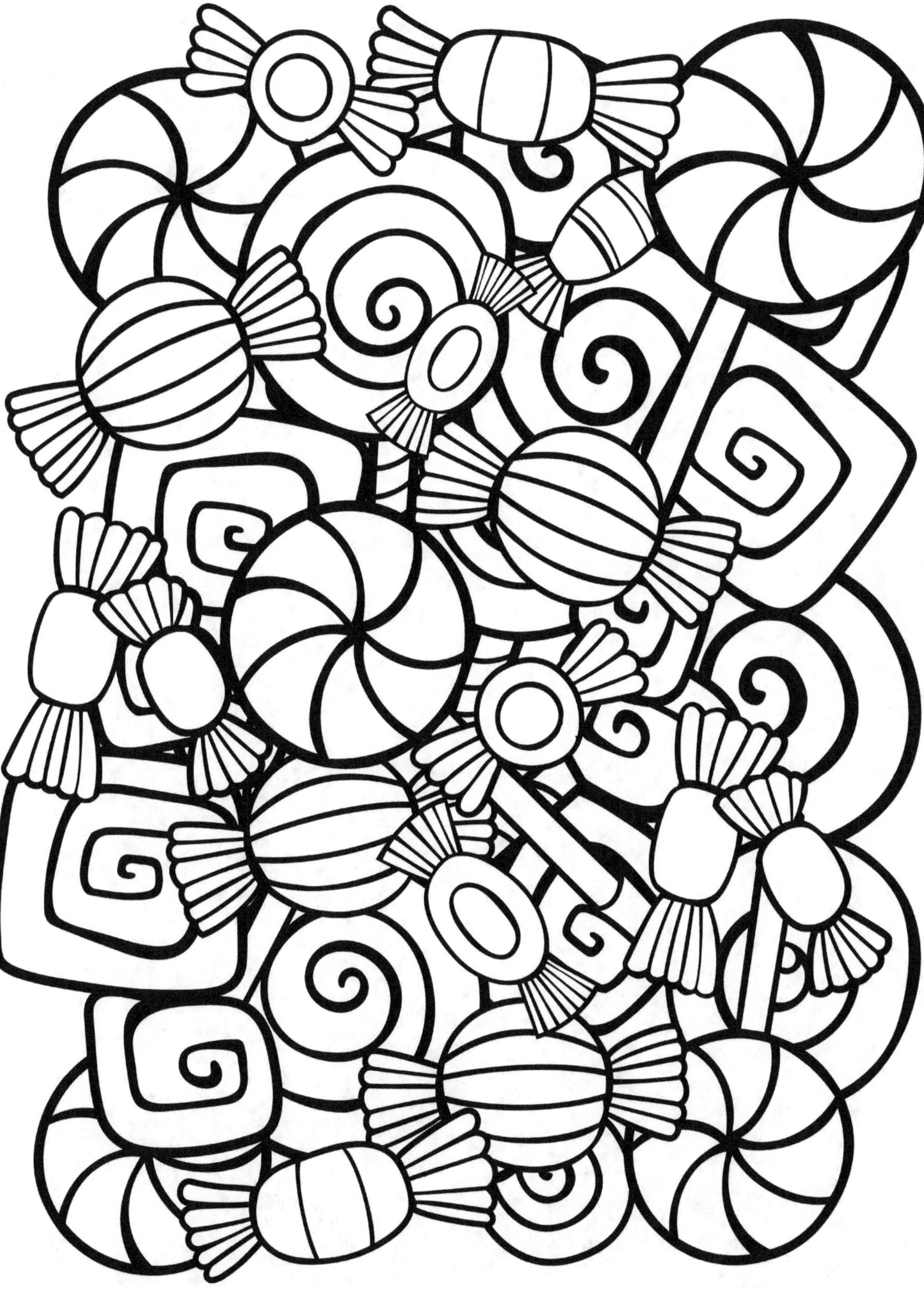

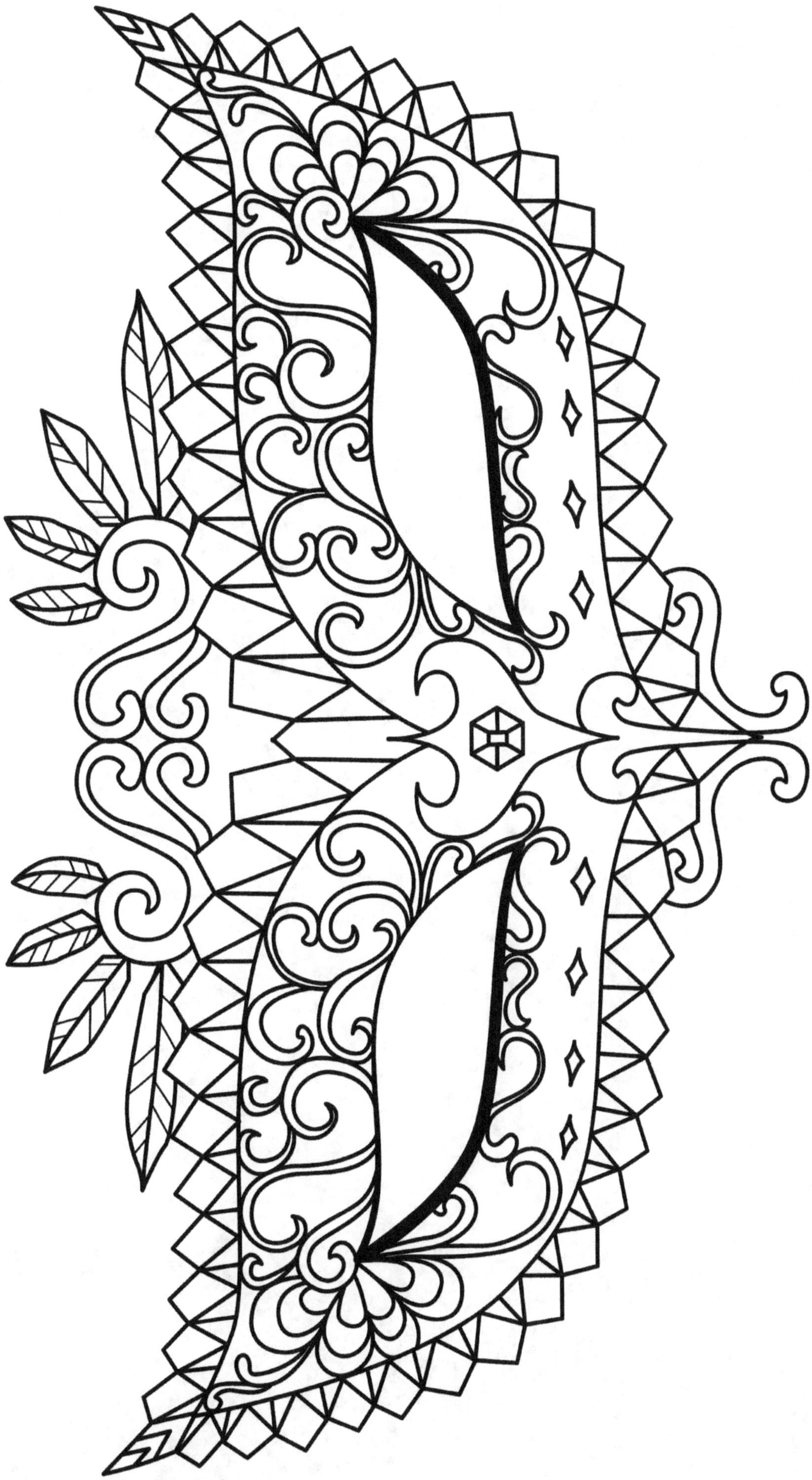

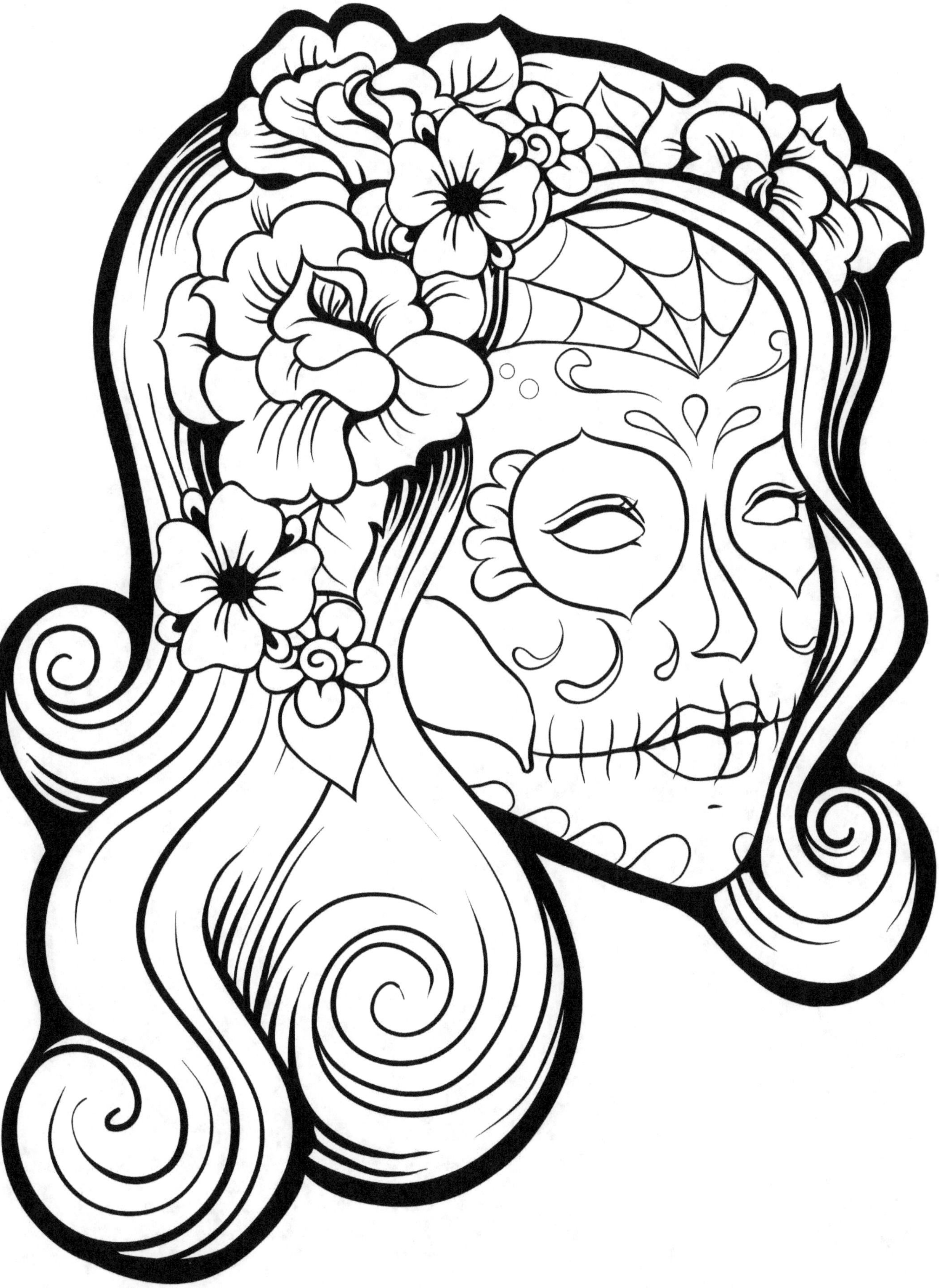

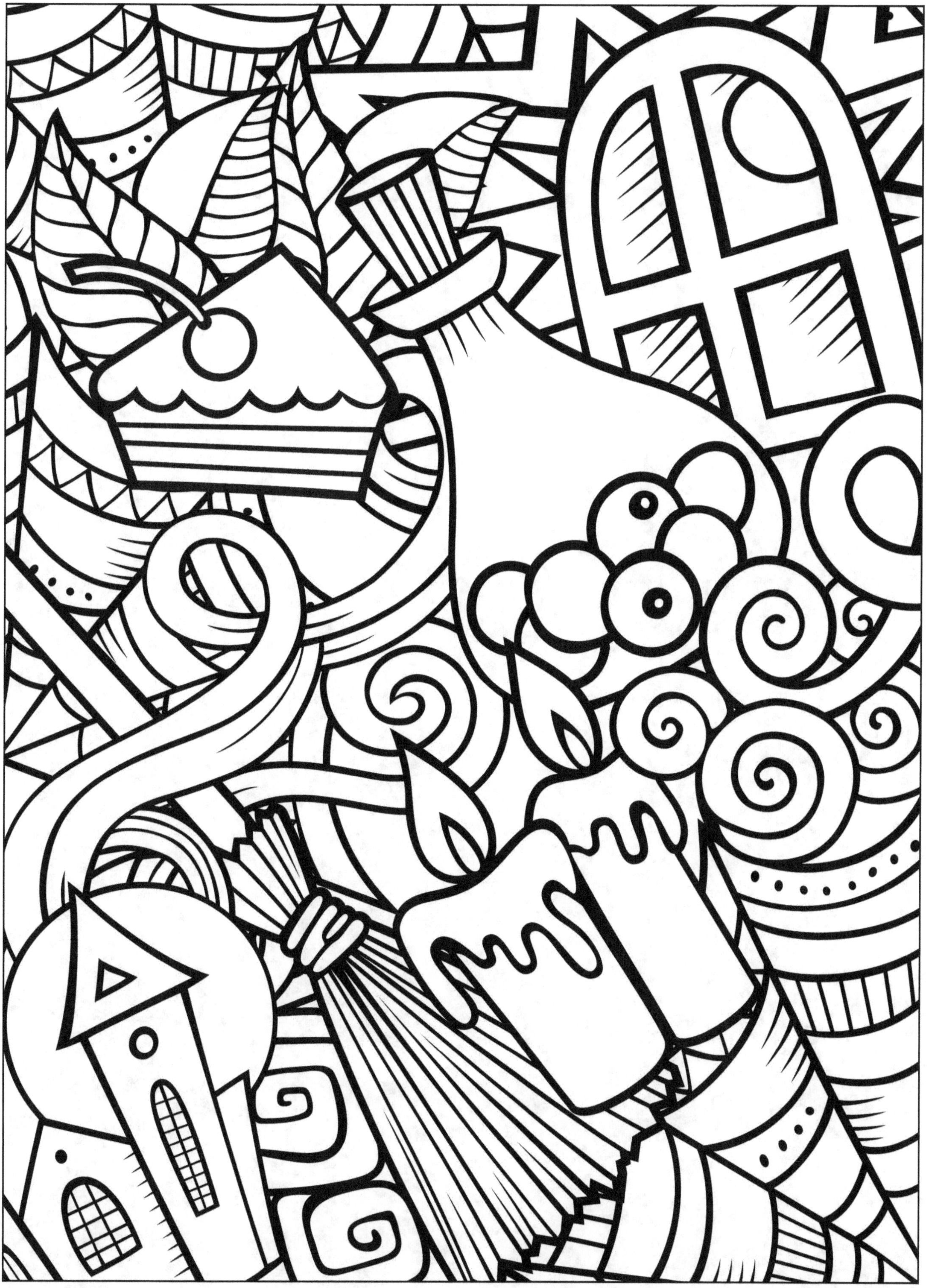

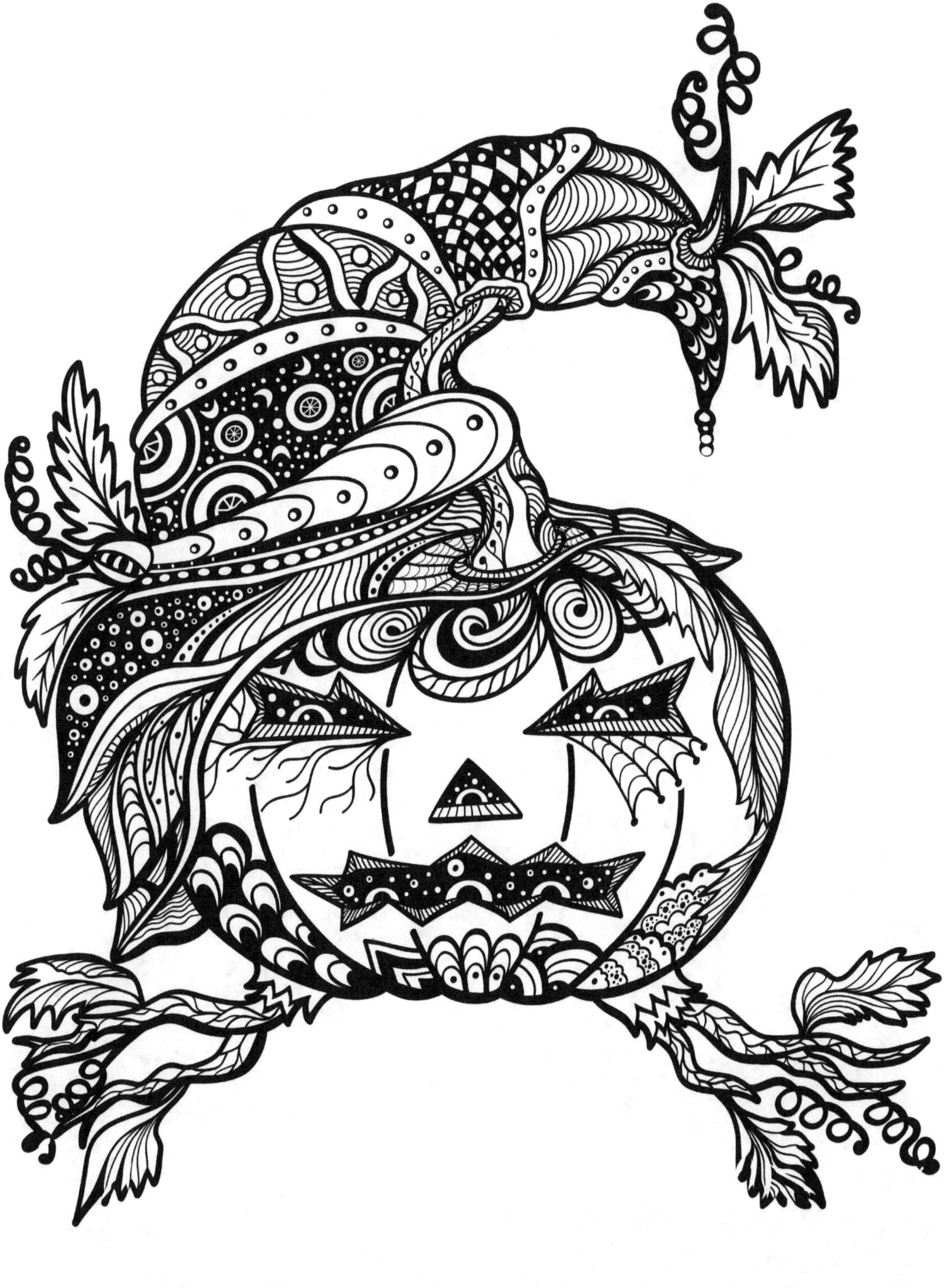

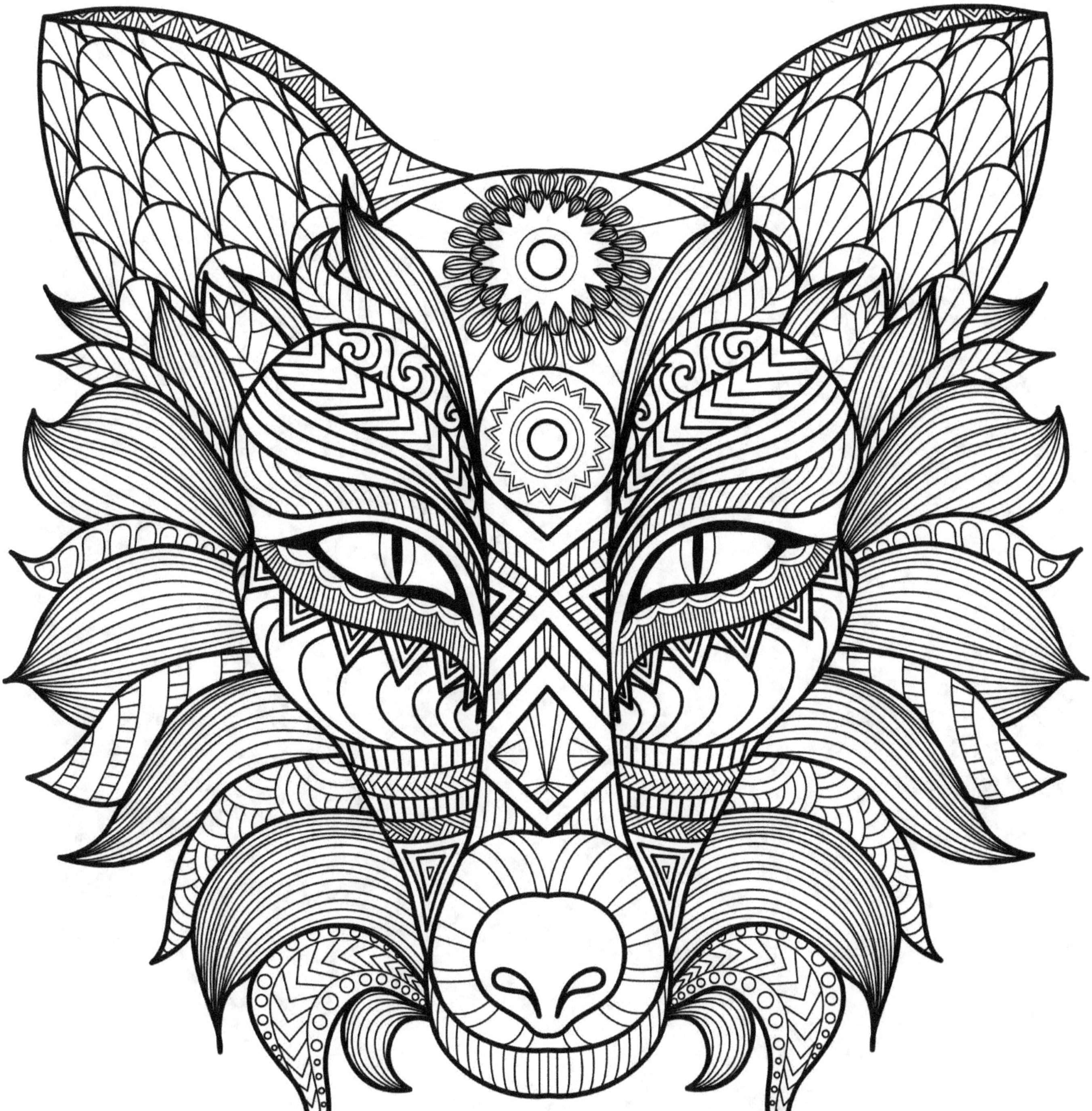

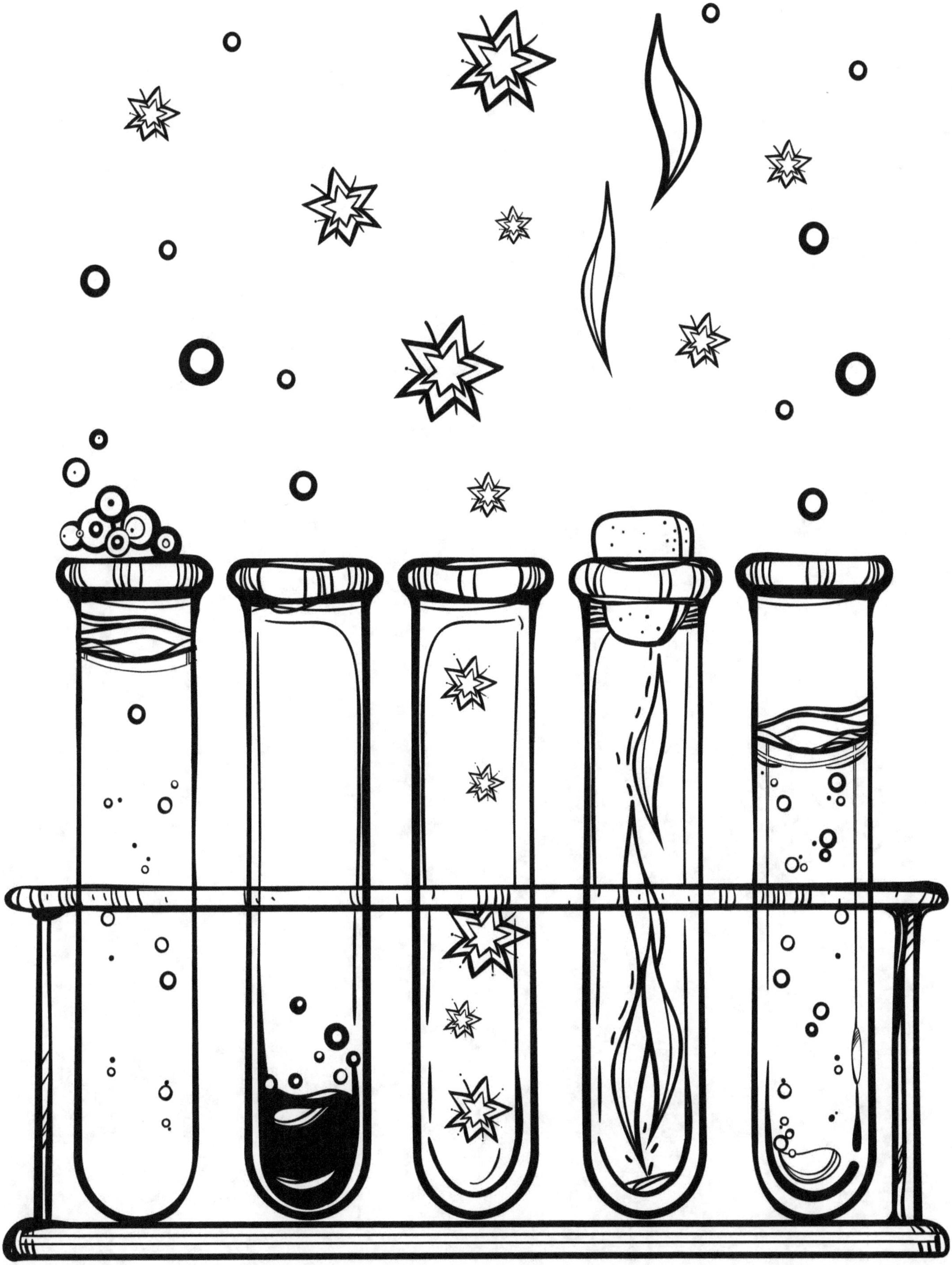

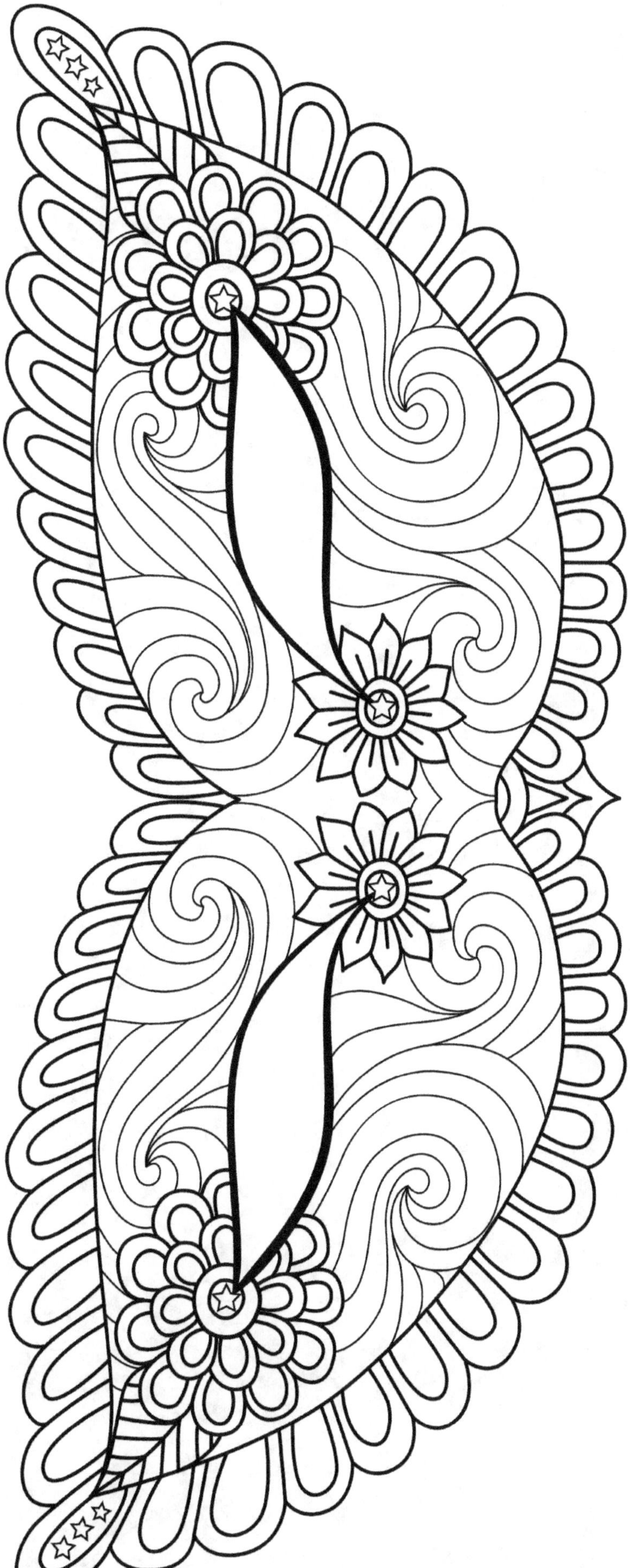

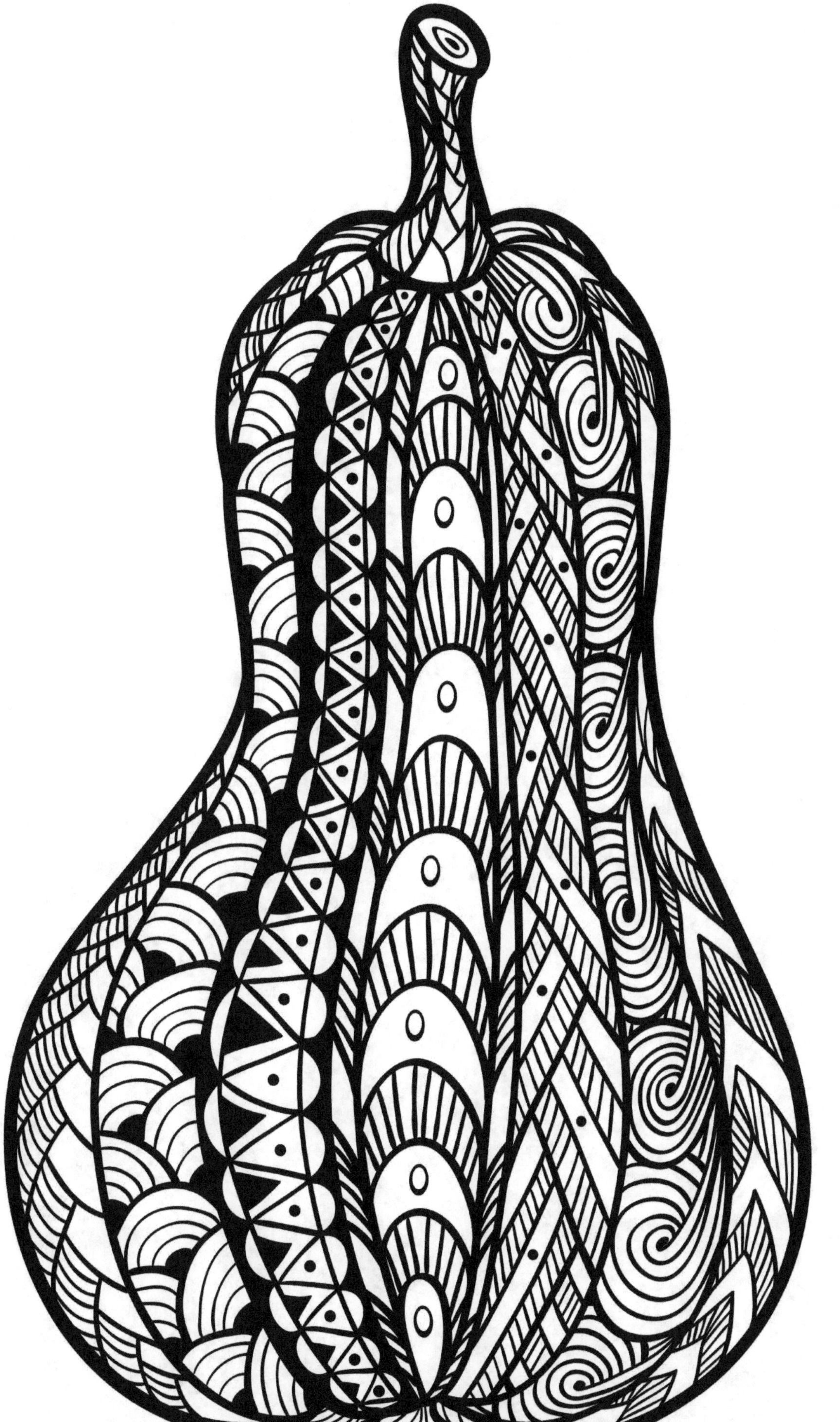

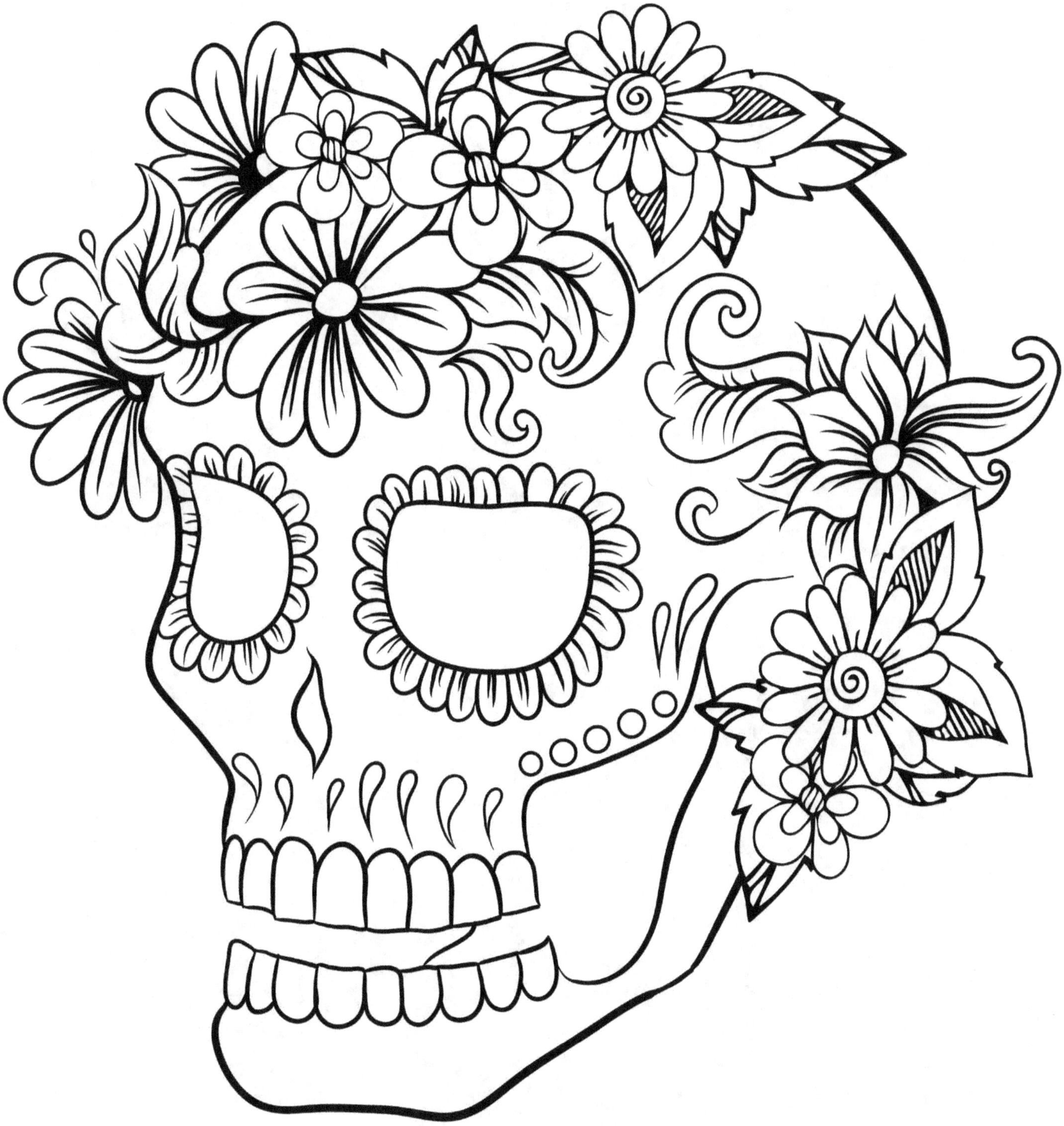

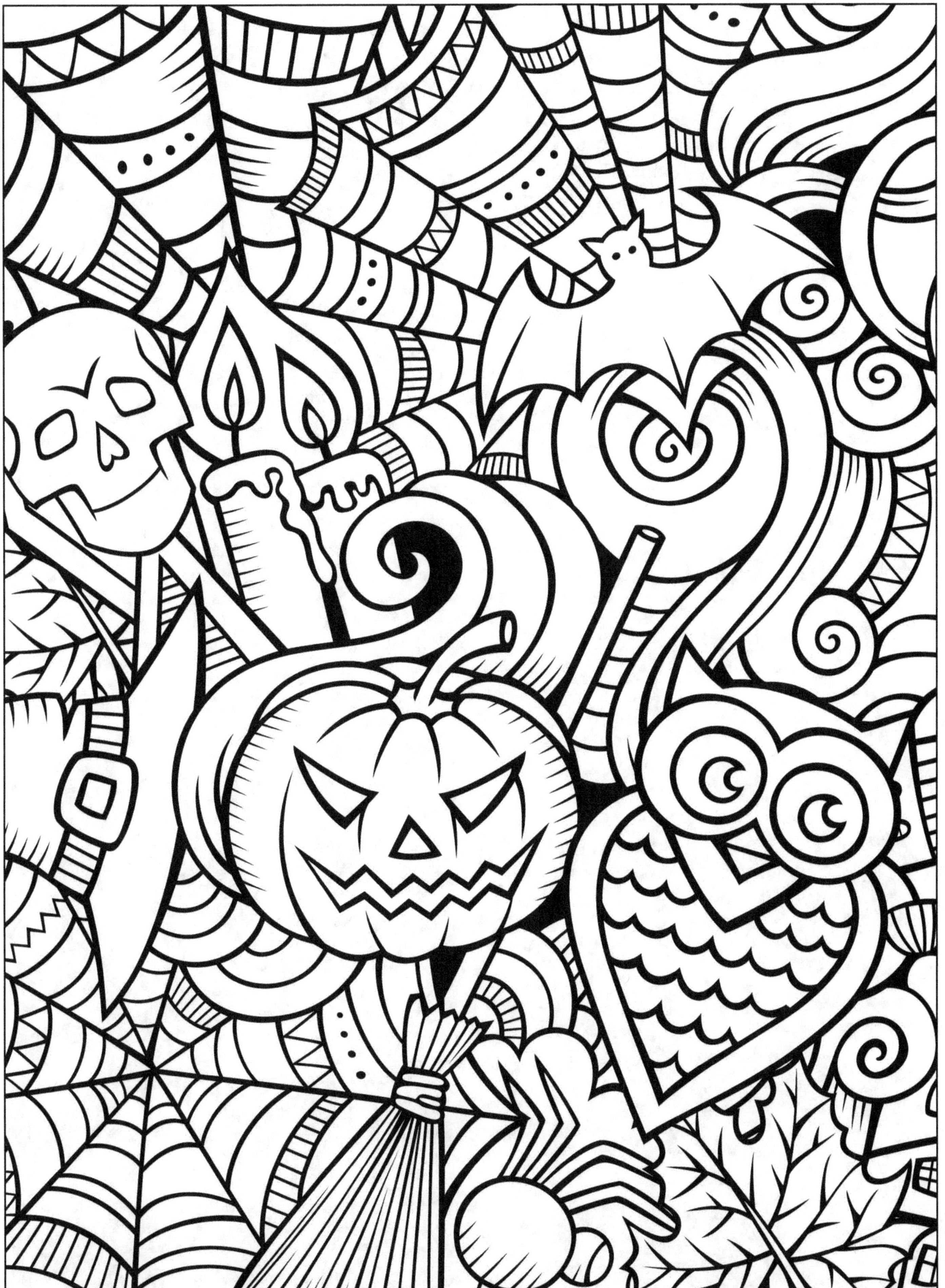

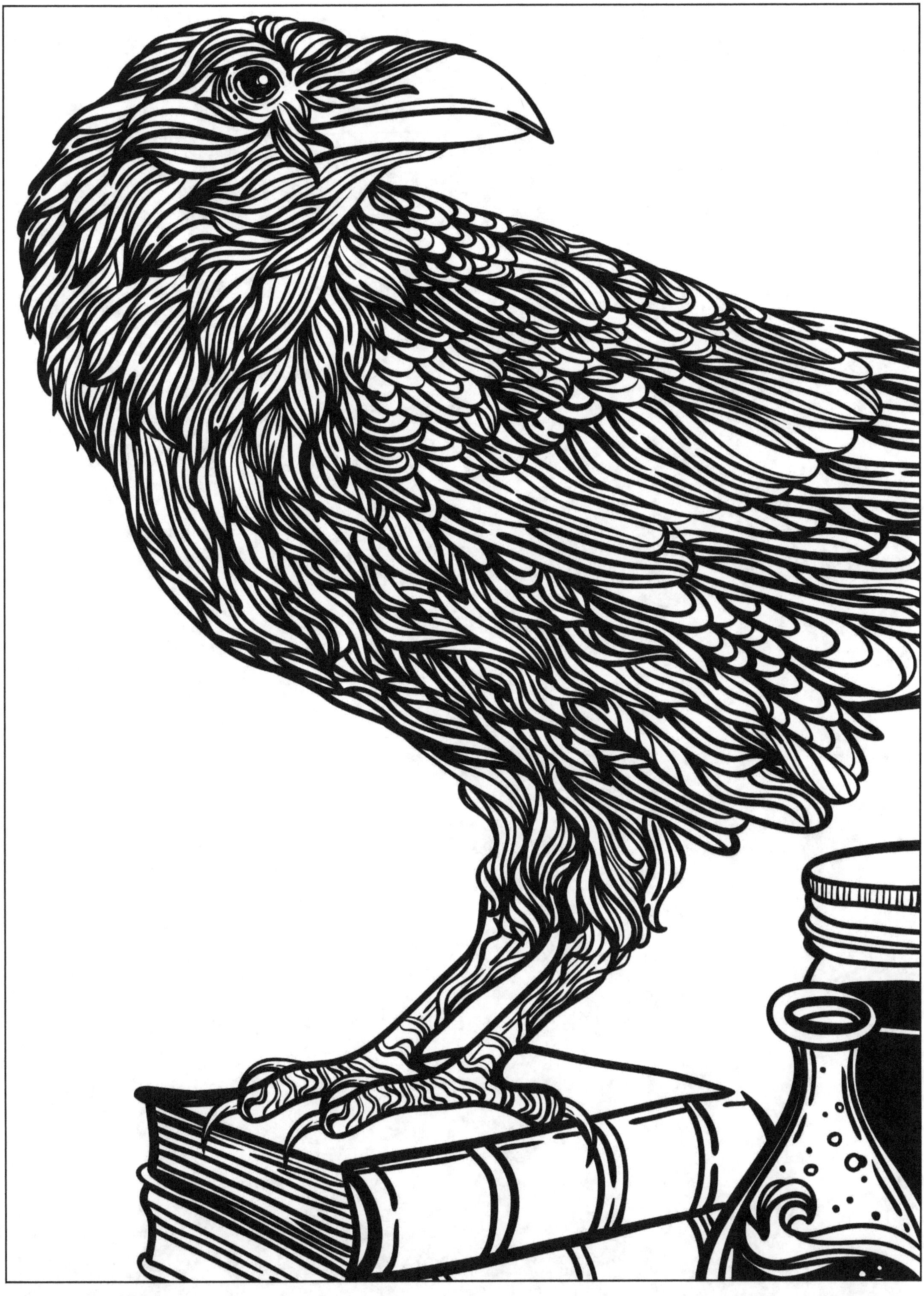

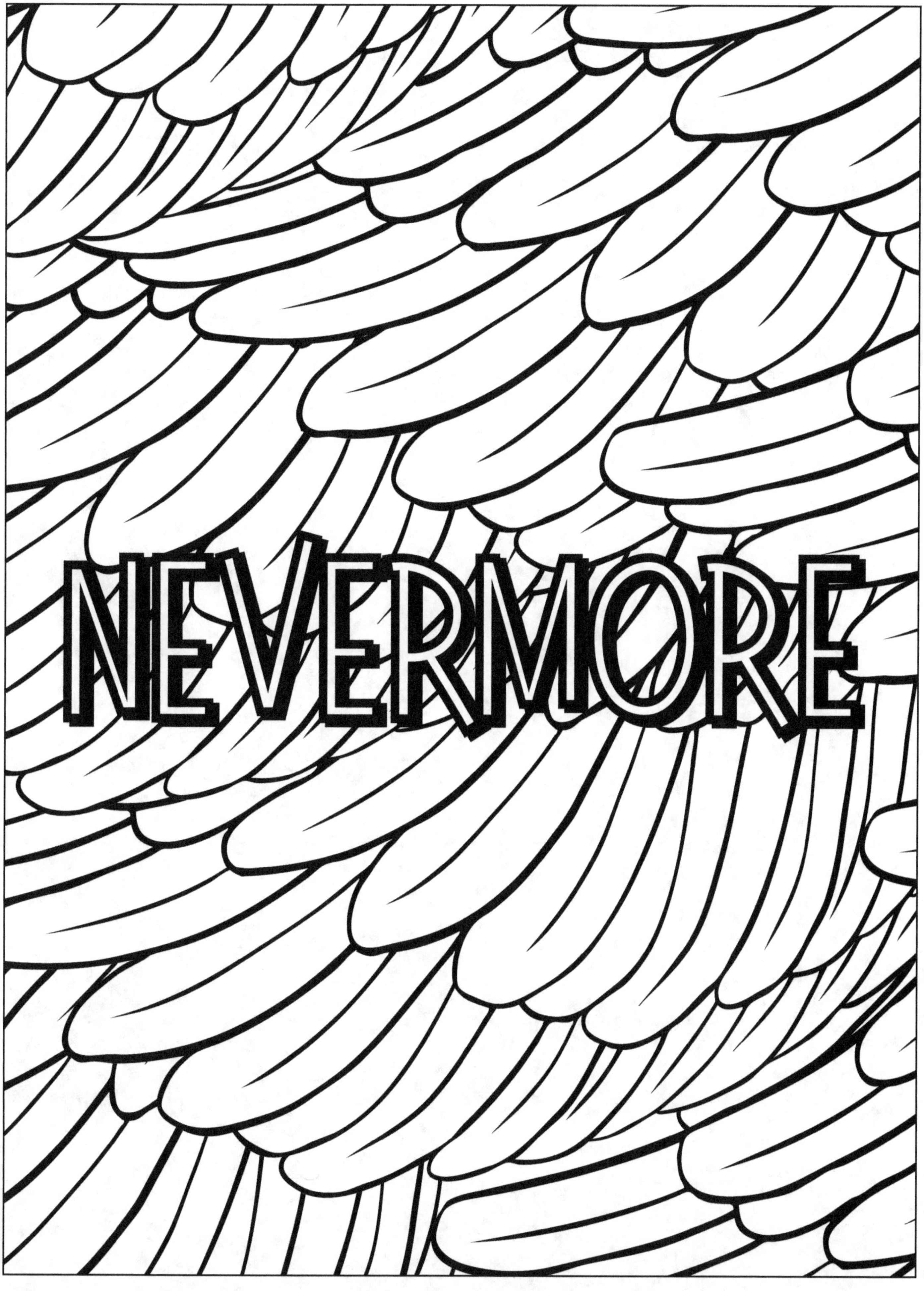
NEVERMORE

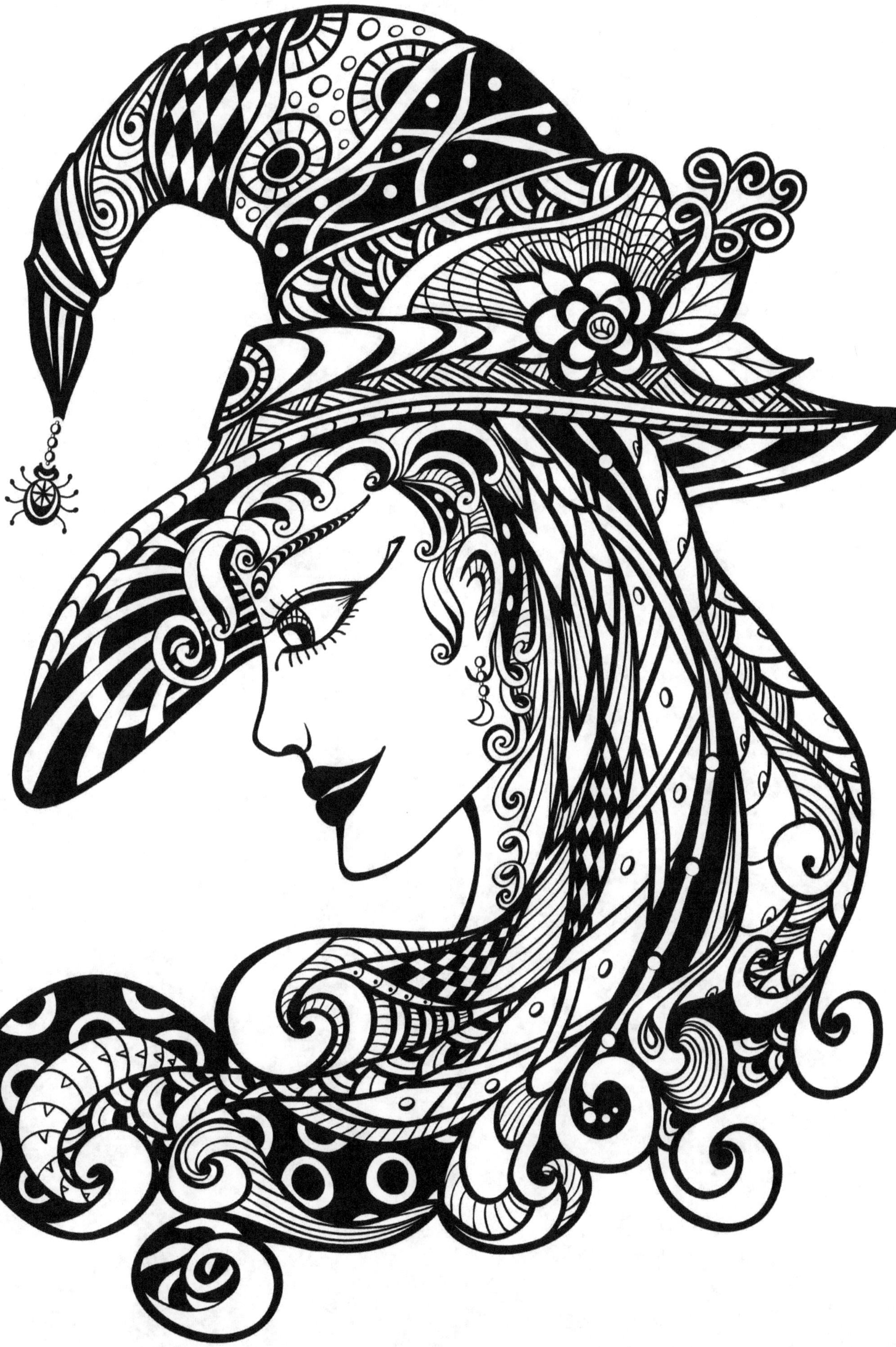

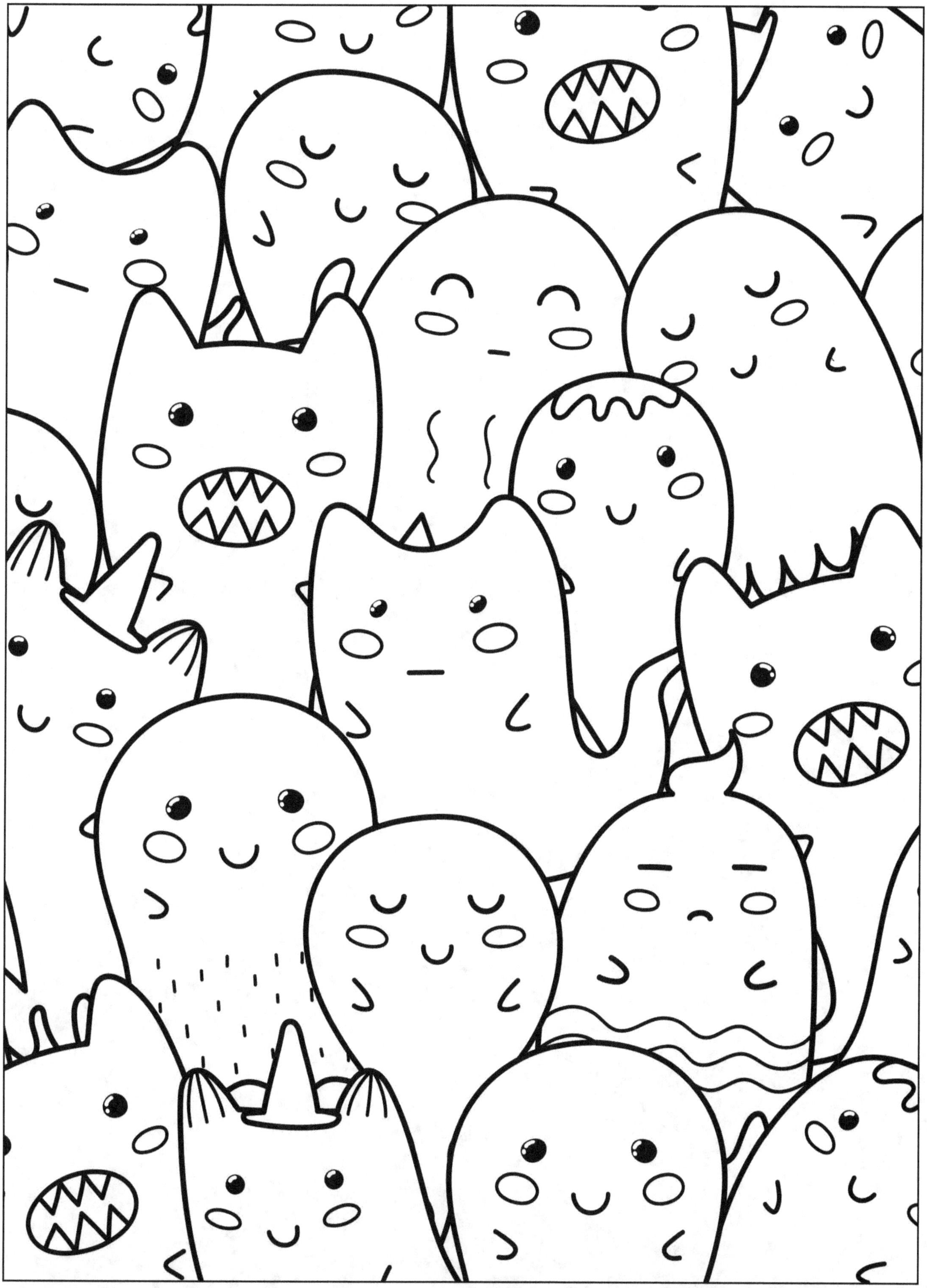

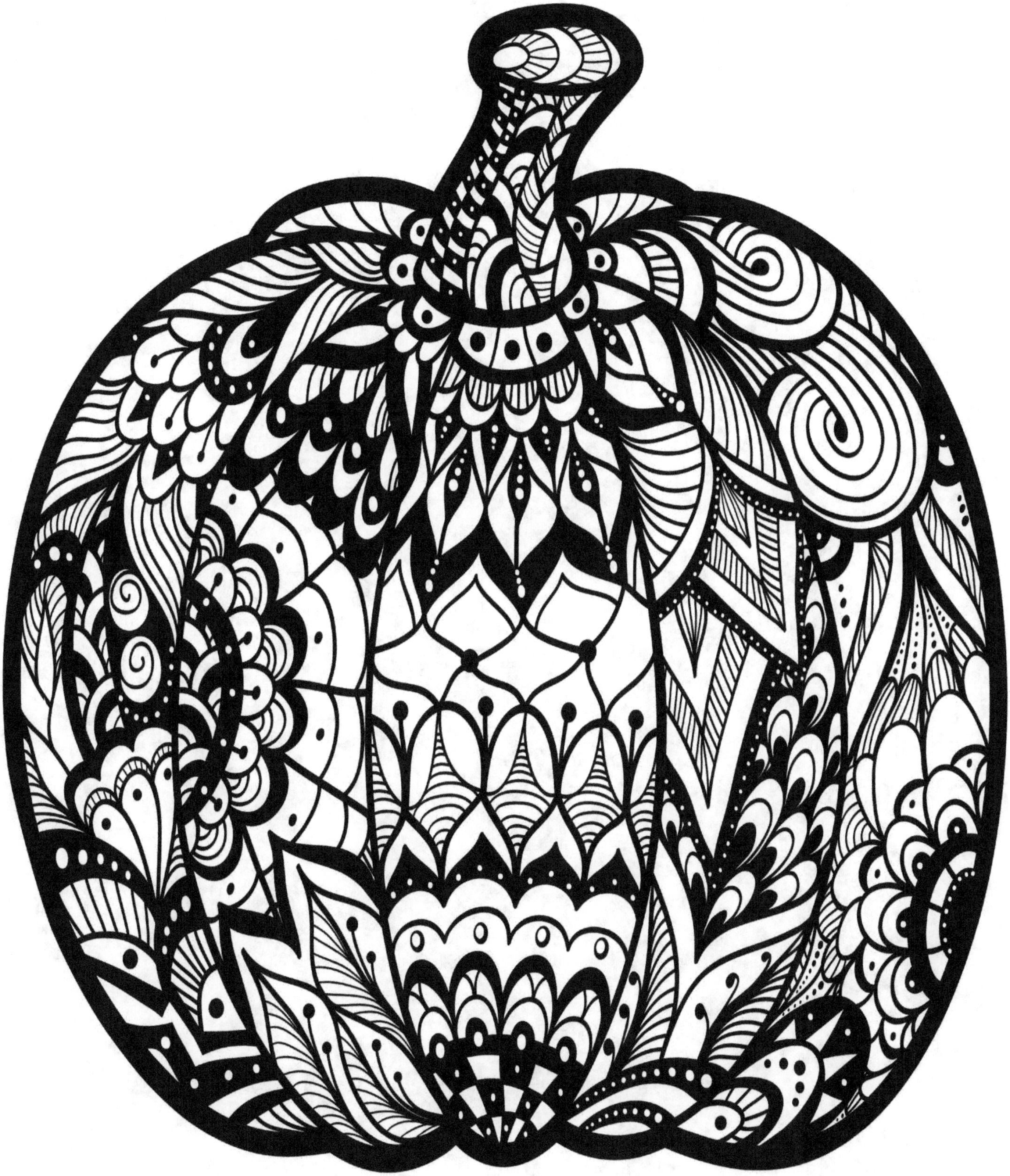

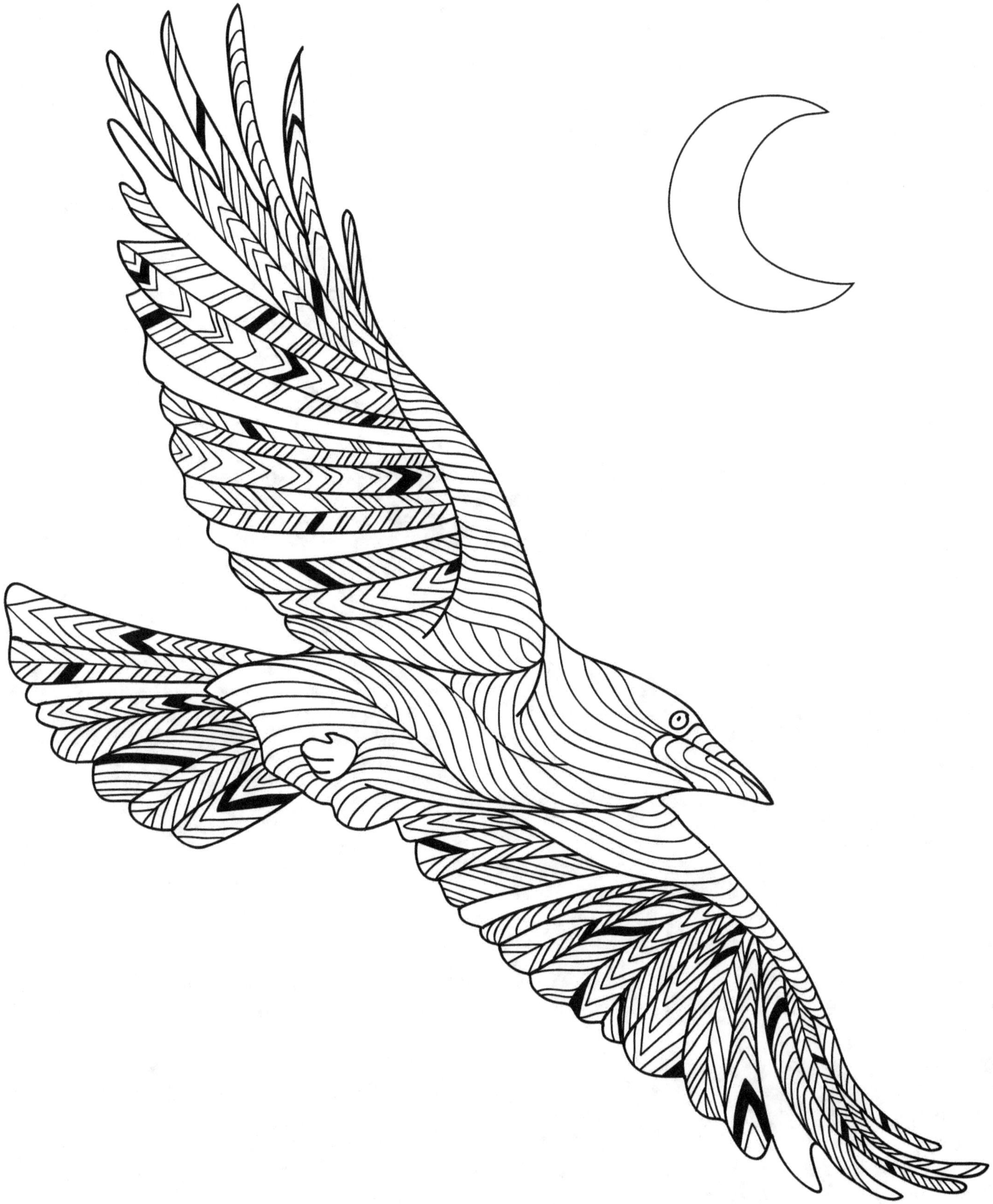

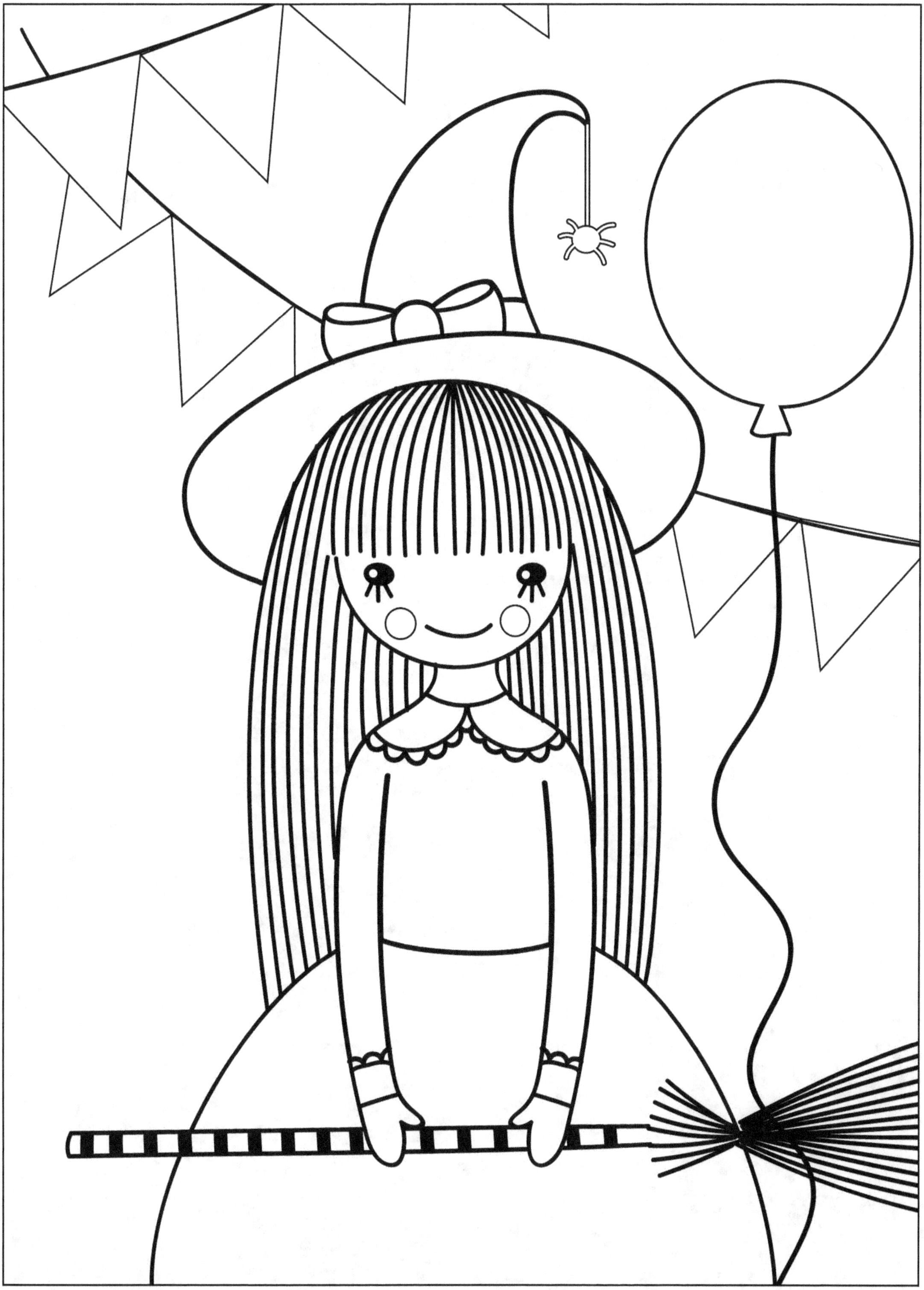

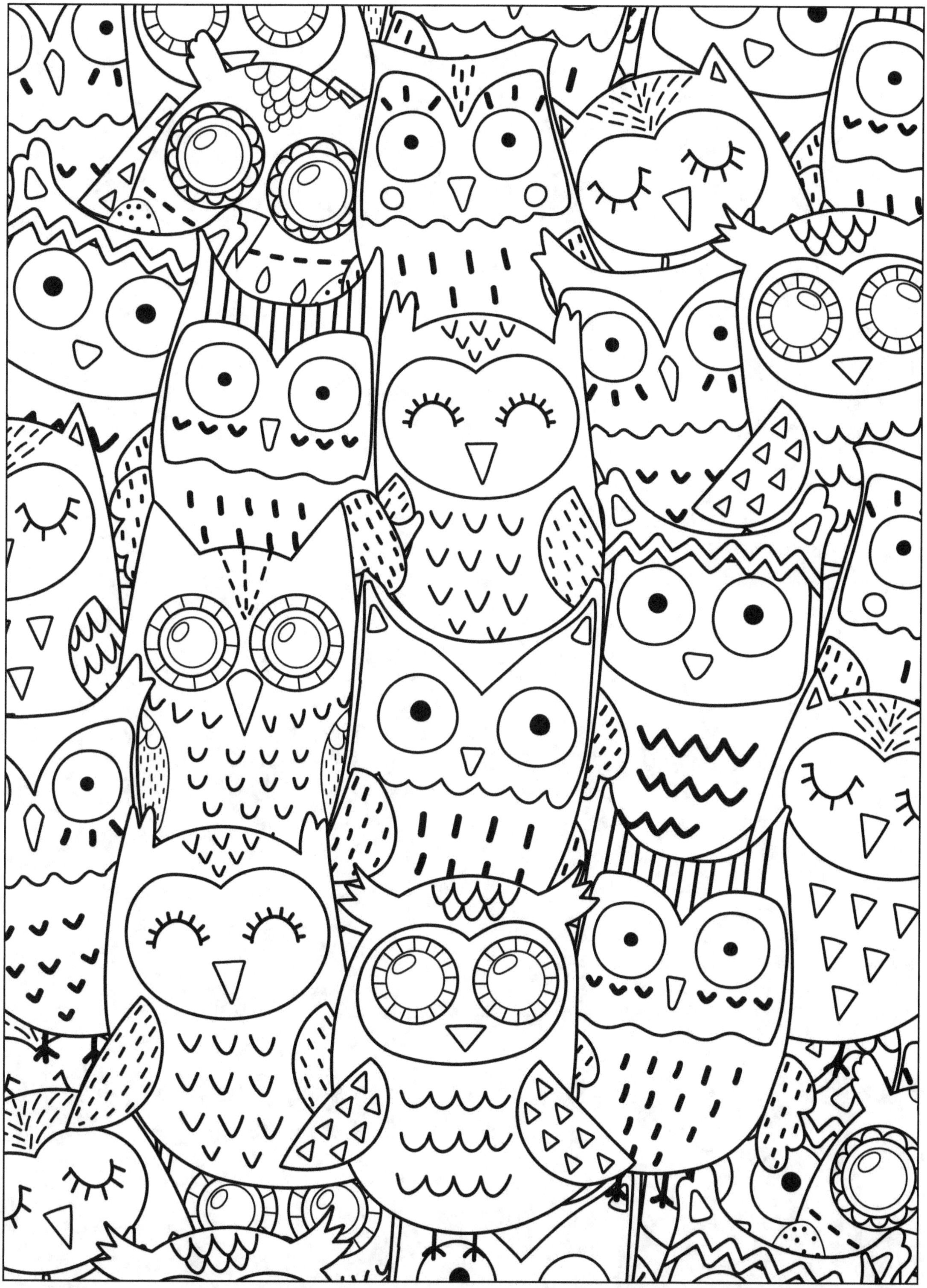

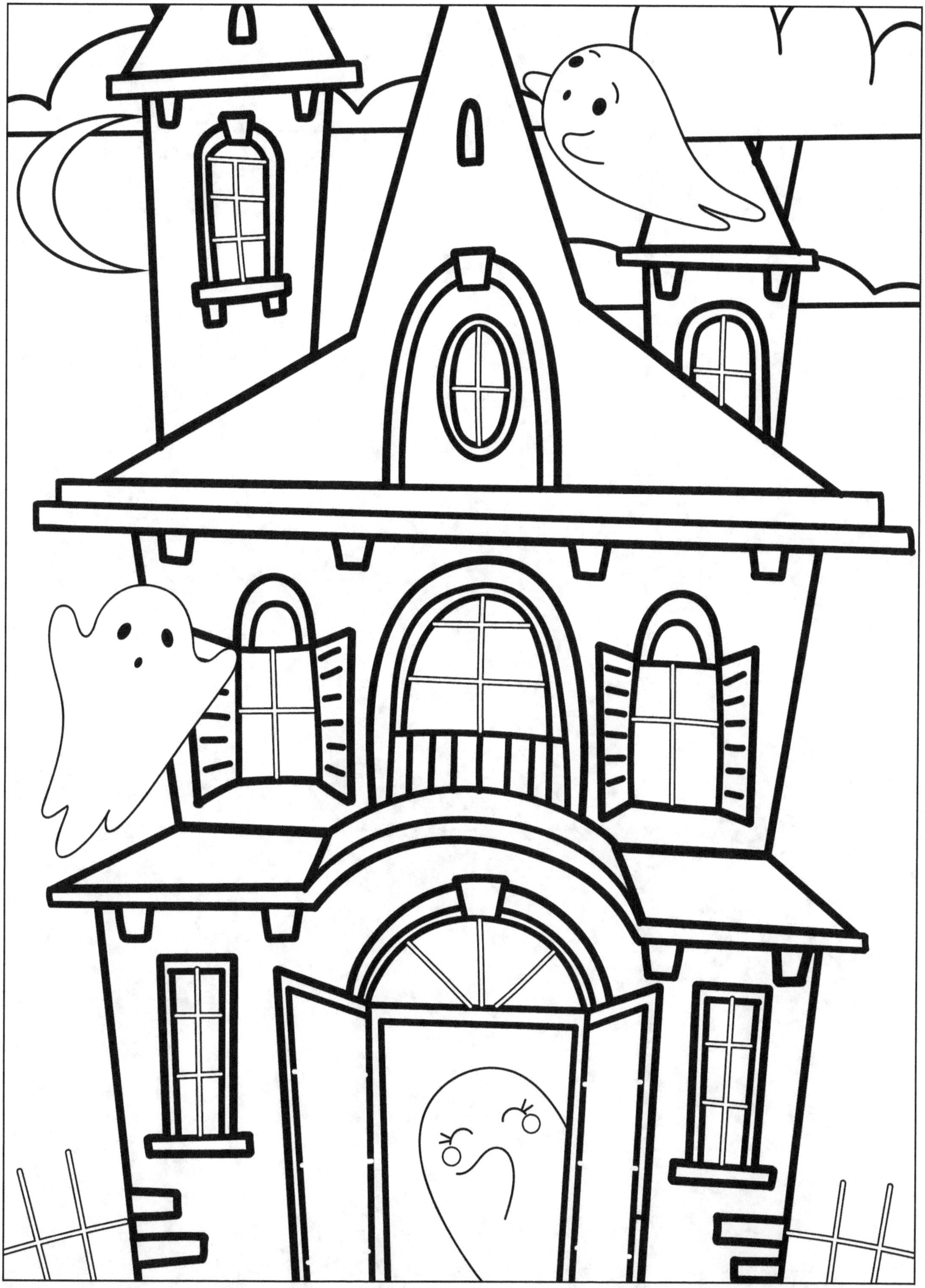

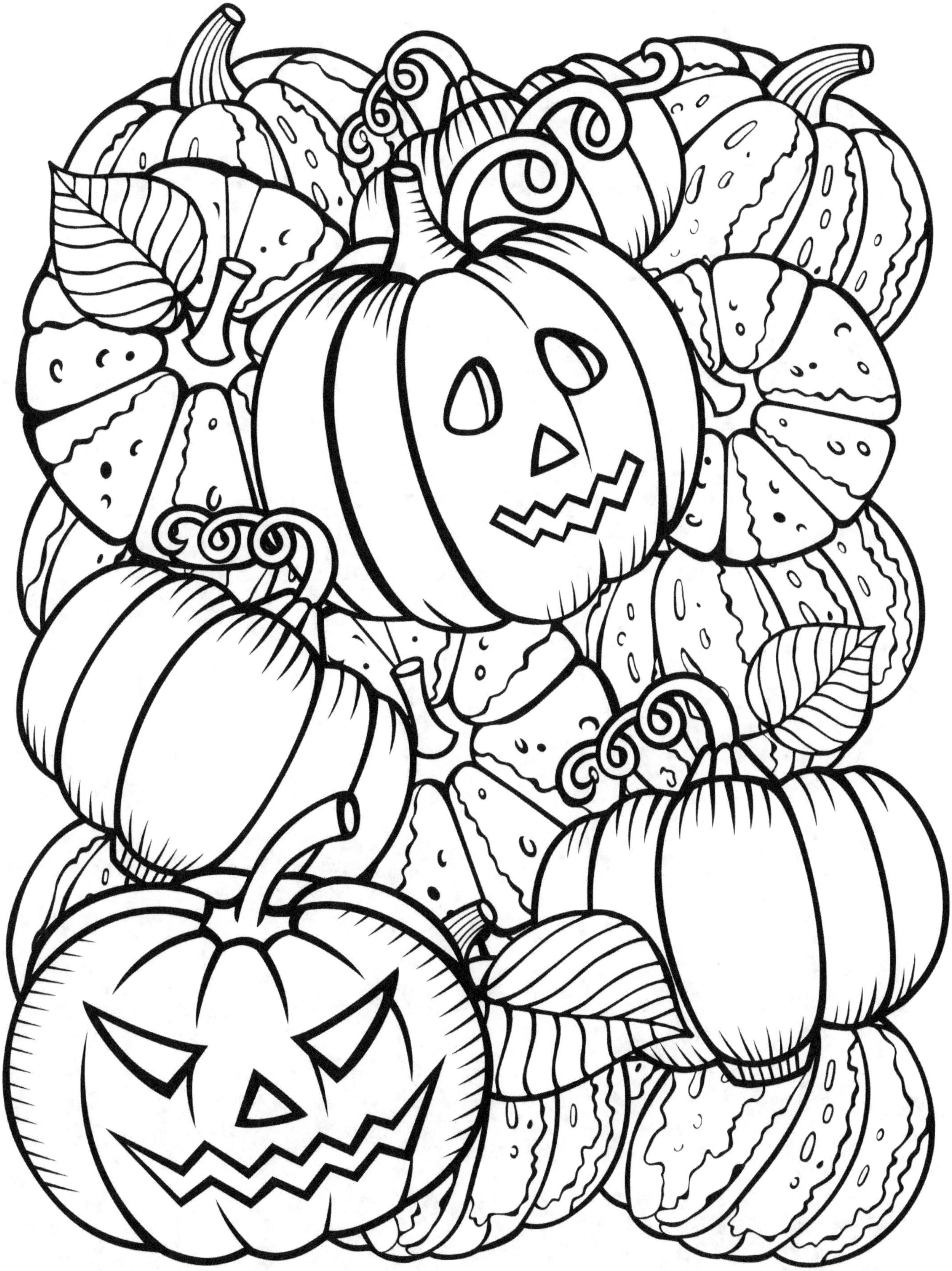

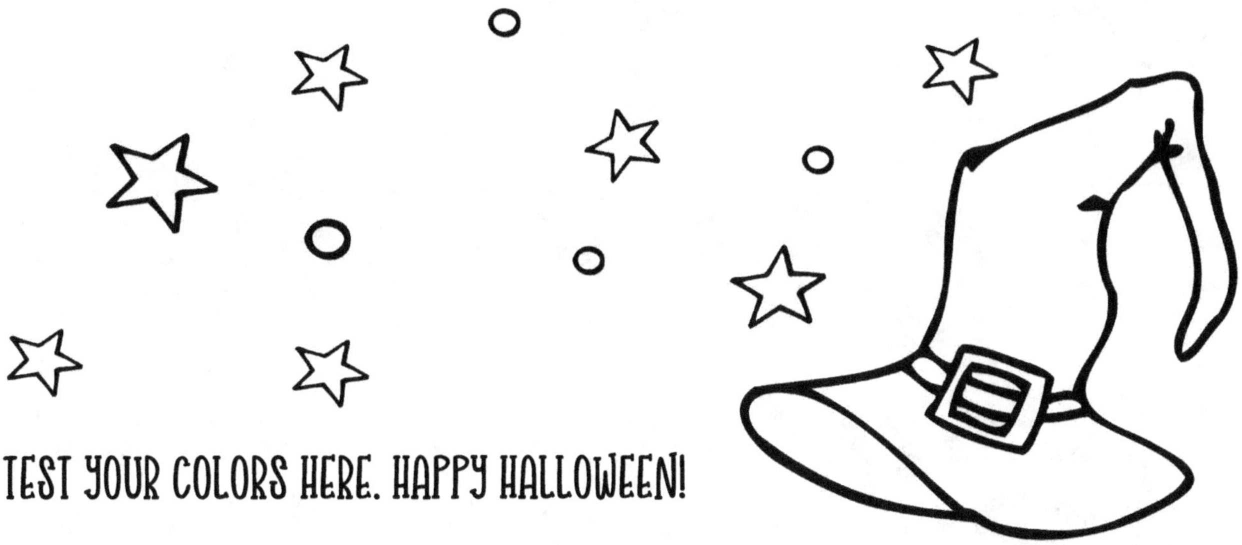

TEST YOUR COLORS HERE. HAPPY HALLOWEEN!

www.ingramcontent.com/pod-product-compliance
Lightning Source LLC
Chambersburg PA
CBHW081739220526
45468CB00008B/2166